"Bob's book is entertaining and funny with its stories about Moe and informative at a level that will attract the attention of competitors on professional tours—especially with regard to what they call 'the zone,' the state of mind where all goes well and the shots fly true."

—**Craig Shankland**, "Top 50 Teacher" by *Golf Digest*

"I was hitting balls on the range one day and Bob walked over and watched me for a few shots. Then in a minute or two, he told me what to do to set up the shot and turn away from the ball. I did it and hit the best 6 iron shot I've ever hit. It was easy."

—**Craig Kwongsee**, Director of Golf at Katchiwano G.C., Lakefield,Ontario, Canada

"I started reading the book and I couldn't put it down. It's great."

—**John Elwood**, an average casual golfer

"I usually shoot in the low 90s. Bob explained by phone a simple way to create the image of the shot-to-be. I did it the next time out and made four birdies and shot 80."

—**Jimi Merk**, a weekend casual golfer

MIND GOLF

THE TROUBLED GENIUS OF MOE NORMAN

Robert Ragland Young

SAVIO
REPVBLIC

A SAVIO REPUBLIC BOOK
An Imprint of Post Hill Press
ISBN: 978-1-63758-798-0
ISBN (eBook): 978-1-63758-799-7

Mind Golf:
The Troubled Genius of Moe Norman
© 2023 by Robert Ragland Young
All Rights Reserved

Cover Designer: Diane Marshall
Illustrator: Diane Marshall
Interior Designer: Yoni Limor
Photographs by: Jan Conner

This is a work of nonfiction. All people, locations, events, and situation are portrayed to the best of the author's memory.

posthillpress.com
New York • Nashville
Published in the United States of America

1 2 3 4 5 6 7 8 9 10

Printed in Canada

My brother, Neil Young, whose encouragement and financial support caused ease in my lengthy association with Moe Norman and, my parents, Scott and Rassy, who drove me to golf tournament as a teenager making it possible for me to get into the great game of golf.

CONTENTS

FOREWORD
by NEIL YOUNG

Our family was always connected to golf. My dad and mom played regularly. Maybe my mom more than my dad for the social aspects of playing with friends, but we were always connected to golf courses in some way. During my youth, we were members at the Summit Golf Club near Toronto, not far from our home in North York. I was going to school as a young boy, and every weekend we visited Summit and played golf.

I remember the eighteenth hole at Summit was viewed by a gallery from the hill outside the clubhouse. Moms, dads, and families all looked down from a big hill where the clubhouse restaurant was located with an outdoor area for drinking, eating, and talking with friends as they spent hours watching players finish on the eighteenth. My mom always talked about how she was so proud of my "short game" chipping and putting. She would gather with her friends up there on the hill and watch as we came up the eighteenth toward the green. I was okay but not really that good. Not like my brother Bob. He seemed to be a "natural" and was already playing in the 70s while I was trying to break 100.

We played a lot of golf during those pre-teen years, eventually moving to a town outside of Toronto called Pickering. Pickering Golf Club was a public course where I played a lot, and my brother played a lot more. Our new house was right across the road. At that time, Bob was really good and was starting to play in junior tournaments.

When our family broke up with mom and dad divorcing, I went to Winnipeg with my mom while Bob stayed in Toronto. My mom and I joined the Winnipeg Canoe Club, where she had played golf as a young girl, then we joined Niakwa Country Club, and I resumed playing on weekends. I was also starting to play in my band, The Squires, and working weekends at the community clubs in town, playing dances, and eventually I sold my clubs to buy a better guitar.

One summer, Bob visited Winnipeg from Toronto, and we talked a lot about what we were going to be doing with our lives. He wanted to be a pro golfer. He was really good and could easily take that on. I could see that.

Bob suggested I stick with music, so eventually I went south to Hollywood with my friends and started a band, Buffalo Springfield, that was successful and got a recording contract. I was writing songs and started to make some money. About that time, I helped Bob get onto the pro-circuit in Canada, in Florida in the winter, and Australia, by sponsoring him. He was great, and it was a good feeling to be part of his success.

Along the way, Bob had met a golfer named Moe Norman, who was quite an amazing player. They became friends and played often together, practicing daily hitting balls for hours at a private practice area down in Florida. Bob had discovered Florida early when our family went down there for winters, and my dad would write in a cabin on the beach we rented. Bob and I juggled schools and got used to moving. We never stopped.

Bob and Moe played together for years; Moe's way of playing was known to be exceptional by all the pros. He really knew how to hit the ball *exactly* where he wanted it to go.

While I kept playing my guitar, Bob kept playing golf. He got to know Moe Norman as well or better than anyone on the planet. Once, Moe told Bob that hitting a shot was like creating music. There is a moment where you just visualize what you want to do and let it happen—not thinking, but there was a lot more to it than that. Bob learned Moe's secrets while he shared his own with Moe.

This book tells the story of Bob and Moe from Bob's view. Bob was closer to Moe than anyone on the planet during those times. Moe was seen as being apparently mildly autistic and very unique in his life and habits. Bob's closeness to him was unusual, unique. Moe Norman was a master of the game, and Bob spent more time with him than anyone for years and years. Bob shares his time with Moe and their golfing secrets in this book. If you love golf, you will find this quite fascinating.

—Neil Young

FOREWORD
by BARRY MORROW

People find their way to golf in any number of ways, and I was no exception. But baseball, back in 1960, was the love of my life, and all you needed then to participate in the national pastime was a glove, any old glove, and a cap on your head. With just that, I could walk out my front door and join a game in progress right there in the street.

There were no public golf courses anywhere near where I lived, so for me, golf was something that dwelled only inside our TV console, when it was working. Even in black & white, seeing swash-buckling Arnie and his raucous army charging over hill and dale was captivating. But the idea of me actually playing the game remained an exotic, faraway notion, as remote as men walking on the moon. "One day, I'll get some clubs and play golf," I told myself.

Time, they say, flies, and three decades later, I landed in Austin, Texas to stay with an old pal for my first golf lesson. In the intervening years, I had switched my dream of pitching in the majors to pitching movie ideas around Hollywood. I'd found success there, perhaps more than my due, creating character-based TV and film dramas about outsiders and underdogs. I was taking a well-deserved break now to play golf.

My host was no teacher, but he did live on a golf course and merely had to step across his patio to be on the 13th tee-box. I woke up early, eager to start the day, while my ersatz instructor slept in. And that's when I spotted it lying there on his coffee table—that 1995 *Golf Digest* magazine with a snow-haired bear of a man on the cover, along with these words: "Moe Knows What Nobody Else Knows."

Moe Norman, I learned, was not only a golfer of extraordinary talent, but a truly odd and eccentric character, an outsider who marched to his own drumbeat. His friends, the piece said, called him the Rain Man of golf. Hooked now, I quickly consumed that article along with a bagel, then strode to the 13th tee-box, laying the magazine open on the ground so I could mimic Moe's swing techniques from the photographs.

How did I do? Not so good. I would need more than photos to find out what Moe knew about golf. Indeed, I'd have to see him in person, and on his home turf preferably, in Canada. Texas, meanwhile, woke up and came out to join me. "You're fired," I told him. "I got a new teacher."

Pursuing Moe became my obsession, and not just for the sake of prying open his golf secrets. The screenwriter in me had to know all about the man himself—how he dreamed and how he saw the world; what made him tick. Was he truly a gifted savant like the role Dustin Hoffman immortalized, but with golf clubs rather than card-counting or toothpicks? I'm certain of one thing—both were excellent drivers.

Somehow, I pulled it all off. I interviewed Moe over the course of a week, then spent another year crafting a story and wrangling with studio lawyers over contracts and other details that aren't important until they are. It was about then that I received an email, or maybe it was a letter in those days. In any case, it was from one Bob Young, who suggested we talk. About Moe.

Mind you, I had written a forgettable TV movie earlier in my career featuring an adolescent Drew Barrymore and Robert (call me Bob) Young, the beloved star of the long-running TV series Father Knows Best. What on Earth, I wondered, might he have to offer about Moe?

That deep, gravelly voice answering the phone sounded nothing like the actor I once knew, nor was it. Rather, it was the son of a legendary sports journalist, brother of a legendary rock-and-roller, and longtime pal of a legendary ball striker. It was that other Bob Young, former Canadian pro golfer, and he launched into a description of what he and Moe had been working on over the course of their friendship—not just the techniques or mechanics of golf, but something far more critical and elusive: the mind. He wanted to take me on a tour of Moe's mind.

I was no golfer, remember, so when Bob spoke of "seeing" the apex of the ball flight before it was struck, or "feeling" the flow of energy in the release, and other nuances of Moe's "inner" game, I knew I was in over my head. "Bob," I said. "You're gonna have to show me."

Bob Young had spent untold hours over the years both playing with Moe and experimenting with him side-by-side on the driving range. Now it was my turn to learn. We got together, first in L.A., then in Toronto, for impromptu lessons, and we talked (I mostly listened) way more than we hit balls, for Bob was now introducing me to Moe's inner process. To hear him tell it, Moe was forever trying to find ways to explain what was in his head. That is, reveal the mental side of golf. Being inherently shy, it didn't come naturally to Moe, but this is where Bob's encouragement and questioning came into play. Thus, Moe continued to grow, bouncing his ever-evolving ideas off of Bob, who recalls them so vividly in this, his uniquely personal account of those halcyon days, *Mind Golf*. Alas, that movie I mentioned didn't get made—yet. Like golf, timing is always key, so I'll keep working on it. I'm also producing a documentary film about Moe that will be, and I mean this, coming soon! I never became the golfer I hoped to be, but the real takeaway for me are the bonds formed in that pursuit, in this case with the many golf folks I so admired and learned from. So, don't feel sorry for me, I won the Grand Slam. I count Bob Young and the late Moe Norman among my friends, and in this inspiring book, *Mind Golf*, they'll become yours.

—Barry Morrow

INTRODUCTION

Golfers want to hit the ball straight and sink putts. The best players in the game gathered around Moe, including Tiger Woods. They came to watch THE GENIUS and learn the golden thought that made it work. "It's so simple," said Moe, but he didn't know to explain it.

Moe's ball striking expertise had no equal, save that of Ben Hogan, one of golf's all-time greatest players and a profoundly influential ball striker himself. What took time was figuring out what to write that would convey to the reader, the aspiring competitive golfer, and the weekend average player who wanted to improve, a true rendition of my experience with Moe Norman across four decades and what it means for the historical record.

I have been writing actively for about fifty years just for my own amusement. I wasn't trying to publish this book. But I know that the core knowledge here will help everyone, including professionals, play better golf. I never talked about it and I didn't show it to other people.

The genius of Moe Norman was revealed instantly when he hit a shot on the golf course or on the practice fairway when he hit hundreds of shots in succession. The ball went where it was supposed to go the way it was supposed to get there, that is, the exact manifestation or close to it, of the shot he envisioned. The best tournament professionals gathered around when given the opportunity to watch. They came to see the golden move that produced perfection and talk to its owner. The best of the game sought Moe out trying to find the answer to their quest: namely, consistent control of the flight of the ball. Moe could create that reality at will. What I contributed, eventually, is the mental sequence of creating and assembling the components of the image of the shot-to-be. It worked easily. Moe used it, and I have since refined it.

Those great players weren't disappointed with what they saw, but they didn't fully grasp what caused it. They examined Moe's set up, the motion of his body, and his perfect balance, but they couldn't read his mind and tune to the mental process that delivered the perfection they witnessed and desired for themselves. Moe neither tried to hide it from them nor did he know what to say to explain it. Added to that, the onlookers didn't know what questions to ask, even though all of them knew that dependable, repeatable ball striking is mentally driven.

I knew that and I hit hundreds of thousands of balls with Moe over the years and played golf with him for decades. Eventually, I asked the right questions and made the right comments and added Moe's response to the little he had already managed to figure out how to tell me. Moe was not articulate but, fortunately, with me he was not secretive. For instance, one day he said, "You have to have a quiet mind." That was the key in his process of ball striking; it was the mental platform from which he created the shot he wanted to see. To Moe, that was what he always did but others did not know that. Moe protected that quietness in his life and rejected any and all circumstance that intruded on it. He led an insular existence, and he knew he was not the same as others in most respects. He saw the world of business, the conflicts, the wars, the turmoil of human relationships, and he said, "No, not for me," and went to the golf course and the game of golf, and he stayed there. That is the actual Moe Norman story. It blended with my own realization that the golf world was my way out of the mainstream nine-to-five routine that I instinctively avoided.

I have tried to include some more "Moe" stories of my own. Unfortunately, many of the professional and amateur players who knew him have passed away, as has Moe himself. But I believe these stories will appeal to golf players around the world, whether they're professional competitive players or casual weekend golfers.

Moe Norman dedicated his life to the great game of golf—people deserve to know more about him. He was as great a ball striker as Ben Hogan.

One day in the early 1980s, Scott Simpson, a United States Open Champion, brought his friend, a PGA Tour player, to a place in Florida near where Moe and I had a private practice area. Moe watched Scott's friend hitting balls and made a few suggestions. It worked. He won Arnold Palmer's PGA Tour event at Bay Hill in Orlando, Florida that week.

Moe's methodology is not complicated; it is simple. The physical mechanics are not complicated. Neither is the mental construct that initiates the physical motion of the swing. In Moe's mind, it was simple. He was right about that. It is simple, as are a lot of things that are great.

The only way to truly understand Moe would be to have a conversation with him as well as notable golf players (some deceased) including Ben Hogan, Arnold Palmer, Bobby Jones, Ken Venturi, Jackie Burke, Nick Weslock (a multi Canadian Amateur champion and longtime close friend of Moe Norman), Alvie Thompson (a Canadian PGA Champion and putting genius), and perhaps a few others who were close to Moe and some family members.

ACKNOWLEDGMENTS

Many, many people helped my life along the way and assisted in bringing me to a point that caused me to write this book. My father and mother encouraged me and saw that I got to the junior tournaments when I was in high school.

Wilson Paterson, the golf professional at Pickering G.C. that was directly across the street from our family home always helped. I made a little money picking up balls when he gave lessons. Wilson was a good player, but he was a school teacher and couldn't put in the time to really take up competitive golf—but he eventually built and owned what is now called Royal Ashburn G.C. George Clifton, a very hospitable and considerate soul, assisted me when he could. He was a golf pro who loved the game. He made Moe welcome at the golf course.

My brother, Neil, was instrumental in providing funding and encouragement that allowed me a comfortable long-term association with Moe Norman. Moe, for his part, was steadfastly supportive of my efforts to succeed in acquiring the finer points of ball striking. Those efforts culminated in my experience in that field in Oak Hill, Florida, where we practiced and excellence came to me. More on that is in the text of this writing.

I also thank Bridgetta Tomarchio, Wadget PR, CEO, Senior Publicist, Manager. Her consistent constructive energy has been instrumental in finalizing the contract with Post Hill Press.

Diane Marshall, a dear friend of over forty years, is the artist who provided the excellent illustrations for the book. She is also a co-author of my song, "Hey America" which may be in the audio version of this book. Moe did say "it's like music." He meant the creative state of mind in striking golf balls.

Todd Graves, founder of Graves Golf Academy, is a serious driving force in my effort with this book to elevate Moe Norman's expertise, his genius, to the recognition it deserves. You can see Moe Norman's swing on the Graves Golf Academy website and listen to what he has to say. Moe spent a lot of time with Todd in the 1990s, and that brought about the creation of Graves Golf Academy. It is totally dedicated to Moe Norman. Todd learned Moe's swing mechanics. His swing is as close to a duplicate of Moe's swing as it's possible to create. If you want to improve, tune to gravesgolf.com then go to the practice fairway.

Lookout Management, my brother Neil's management company and his manager, Frank Gironda, negotiated the contract with Post Hill Press and participated in many conference calls while we created the marketing plan.

My sincere thanks to Hart Moroney, owner of Tamarac GC in Ennismore, Ontario, for his hospitality and unlimited access to his golf course.

USPGA 2001 Teacher Of The Year, Craig Shankland, provided nineteen years of hosting Moe Norman clinics that helped Moe professionally and financially and contributed significantly to the mystique of Moe Norman that prevails to this day.

My thanks and Moe's thanks to John Elwood for his financial assistance when we needed it in the late 1970s.

I used and understood Moe's mechanics and added to it my perception of the mental construct of ball striking which Moe and I both came to use. It is the core of *Mind Golf*.

CHAPTER 1
A FRUIT JUICE CAN

In the early 1980s, when we played every afternoon at Spruce Creek in South Daytona Beach, I arrived in the parking lot one day to find Moe wandering around with a golf shaft and sticking it in the sand here and there. The parking lot had many, many palmetto bushes in it, but unbeknownst to Moe, it had been revamped overnight and was newly raked and minus a lot of palmettos. It looked very different. Moe kept sticking the shaft in the sand here and there. I looked at him. He said nothing. Finally, I said, "What are you doing?"

He smiled. "Looking for something," he said.

"How much have you got buried here, Moe?"

"Eight, ten thousand. Yup. I'll find it."

It was in a fruit juice can. He found it.

It may be that somewhere in Ontario or Florida in the rough on some fairway somewhere at who knows how many golf courses there is a stash of Moe's money hidden under the ground. This is not an invitation to members of various golf clubs where Moe played to start digging up the rough; however, there are metal detectors like the ones I see on Florida beaches, and if someone finds a can of money at one of those courses, it should be donated to TGR Foundation, a Tiger Woods charity. That idea could be included in the documentary Graves Golf Academy is producing that will be shown, we hope, at the Toronto International Film Festival.

Even if there is no buried treasure, I can talk about this part of Moe's life, and we'll figure out another way to benefit TGR Foundation and the fine things it does. Tiger, you may know, is a serious Moe Norman admirer. He wants to do what Moe and Ben Hogan could do. Golf can be a healing force in today's world. And that is obviously needed. The entertainment industry can be very helpful in furthering this, given its capacity to draw large crowds and raise funds for worthy causes. I have access to that industry.

Perhaps, the most significant comment Moe Norman made about anything was one day at a golf course somewhere in Ontario, Canada. We were talking about what people do. He said, "People don't love each other, they don't know who they are."

He saw life through his own eyes and mental lens, and he lived in his own world. He lived daily with his way of doing things and the years rolled by. He did watch people. He was observant.

"You have eyes, you can see," he would say. "You have ears, you can hear," was his frequent response if asked a question about something. If I hit a great shot on the course and said, "why did that happen, what caused that?" His response was, "you already know why." He knew that some part of me already knew or it couldn't have happened. Then he'd laugh and say, "I'll tell you." It was a little game he played, but he always told me what I needed to know as best he could. When he liked what he saw, he'd say, "whatever you did there." He meant whatever I had in mind.

Competitive golfers and the bedrock loyalist fans like the Graves Golf Academy website membership want to know what Moe Norman was really like—because he was an eccentric creative genius who could control where the ball goes. Moe didn't see himself that way early in life. He just kept hitting balls, millions of them, and he figured it out, at least in the eyes of the observers. In his own mind, he was open to improvement, to refinement, and he achieved that too near the end of his life.

Those who recognized him as a master ball striker may be surprised by his words at age seventy-three, shortly before he died. "All my life," he said, "wrong." What he discovered is contained in the text of this book, *Mind Golf*. It is very revealing and, in my view, will be a significant factor in improving the performance of competitive players on all professional tours. It will help all players, including beginners. Why will it achieve that? The answer is because it is simple. Learn to establish "the ready position" by creating it with the feeling imparted by forming the image of "the-shot-to-be." The technique of forming that image is critical.

When I started playing golf with Moe, I didn't set out to write a book about Moe and me and our decades-long personal association. I was trying to figure out how to hit the ball and have it get to the desired destination. That's it. Moe could do that, but he didn't know what to say to explain how he did it.

Now, I am writing more about my personal relationship with Moe at the request of those who have read the manuscript and feel there is more to Moe Norman than I have revealed. Some of that already exists in the text as "Moe stories," but I want to add what I think is appropriate to establish the fact that Moe Norman's life, his existence, was expressed through his single-minded attachment to the game of golf. This is very well explained by Lloyd Tucker, the golf pro who came to know Moe when Moe went to Rockway Golf Club in Kitchener, Ontario, as a child who wanted to play golf. Here is how he described his perception of Moe Norman to me:

I knew Moe when he was just getting started hitting golf balls at Rockway. And I'd go out there to the practice fairway and all these kids are beating balls in one direction or another, and

I'd watch what they were doing and make suggestions here and there, and I always told them what I say to you keep to yourself and you work on it because it's not the same for everybody. Some people do things better than others and some need more instruction, and it varies from one person to another. So I treated them separately. Well, Moe was definitely separate. There was nobody out there like him. He was dedicated. He hit golf balls, and hit them, and hit them, and hit them again, and picked them up and hit them again. And he was so dedicated that I admired him, this guy is going to do this. And he did. He just kept doing it, and we had a good rapport because he trusted me. He knew that I was trying to help him. Nobody else was. His family didn't do anything. Moe went to the golf course, then he went home and went to bed. He ate food and that was it. I know that when his father died he was in Florida with you, and he came in the spring and said 'where's Dad?' Well, Dad had died and nobody told him. So...his whole existence...was... he was included in the world of golf, reluctantly by some, the Ontario Golf Association and The Royal Canadian Golf Association, and there were some golf pros who felt the same and didn't want him around their golf courses, but a lot did, and Moe was Moe, he did his best, and eventually he bought decent clothes and started to take care of himself on a daily basis so that everywhere he went he could show up and say hello and play a few holes on their golf course with guys from the pro shop, hit some balls, putts, and that was Moe's idea of socializing. He'd cruise around and get out of his car with his putter bouncing a ball on it, and that was his life.

Now when he was young, he was so determined. I admired him, but I also knew this is the only thing this kid knows how to do, he doesn't know how to do anything else. He's an outcast from even his own age group; they didn't know what to do with him either. Moe's that weird kid who got banged on the head in a car accident. So it was tough for him, but he prevailed, he just kept doing what he was doing and eventually he learned how to read. He got a dictionary so he could figure out what words meant. And he read and he was really a very smart individual in a lot of respects, but his view of life was so simple and deep. He just kept to himself and kept his thoughts to himself, and once in a while with someone like you, he expressed himself. You got to know each other. You spent all that time together and hit hundreds of thousands of balls, nobody did that with Moe, not to that degree. The individual from Oklahoma, Todd Graves, spent a lot of time with Moe, but nothing like what you did. And Todd Graves is making a very good business plan of dedicating his website to Moe Norman. But Todd Graves has no idea, except from what he's read of what you've written and shown Moe—if Moe showed him that—of what you know and understand. He will come to understand it by reading what you've written about and what he never delved into with Moe. Moe probably never talked to him about that. Moe just showed him the mechanics, how to hold the club the right way and the basic principles of what he had in mind, how to turn away from the ball, where your weight goes, and so on. He developed that from childhood and got better and better, but he was definitely a rare specimen. This little guy with determination that was unmatched. He was going to be a golfer. He became that. He became a real golfer. The only person compared to Ben Hogan favorably as a striker of golf balls. And those two to this day still hold that title. Nobody hits the ball as well as Moe and Ben Hogan did. The only person whose done that frankly is you. That's what Moe says to me. You may do it again. We are here watching.

Moe's world did not include girlfriends, wives, and his own family with children. Compared to so called "normal," his world was not that; it was abnormal. Moe's world was insular, at least to the observers. His world was golf related, no more and no less. It was limited. He had no political interests, no business interests that were not directly golf related in the form of prize money and, later in life, other golf-related sources. He dealt with the world around himself by avoiding most of it, except for what he liked, and that was limited to his personal world of golf.

Within the boundaries of his golfing domain were those people he liked and with whom he played golf, talked about golf, both professional golf and amateur, and people who helped him cope with what he had to contend with in life and survive. Prominent in that aspect of Moe's existence was the Maue family of Kitchener, Ontario and the Membry family of Gilford, Ontario, both of whom owned golf courses. There were many others including Wilson Paterson of Royal Ashburn G.C. of Ashburn, Ontario, Ken Duggan, Lloyd and Murray Tucker, George Clifton, and golf pros in general. A stalwart and encouraging supporter was Craig Shankland, a prominent teacher of the PGA of America and the LPGA Tour. It was Craig who helped Moe get started doing clinics. Lee Trevino knew Moe and encouraged him. Nick Weslock, a multi-time Canadian Amateur Champion, and Moe were fast friends. Nick was great. He showed me, at Moe's request, some of the finer points of the short game. He was a master. "Nick the Wedge" we called him. It was a term of respect. All who knew Moe knew he was different from other people. That seemed to stem from a car accident at age five when he suffered a head injury. Questions regarding autism and autistic behavior were mentioned but not dwelt upon.

As Moe cruised in his Cadillac from golf course to golf course in Canada and the United States, his talent as a ball striker grew and grew. That was Moe's world. It was good for him, but it was without the life experiences others enjoyed. "They seem to be good for each other," he said of a married couple we both knew. So, Moe saw the part of life in which he had no direct engagement. I think he wondered what his life would have been like had he lived the way others did with children going to school and growing up, but he knew it wasn't for him. He was a nomad, on the road, perpetually on the road, just like traveling musicians. "On the Road Again" is the song. Moe traveled down that road singing along with Frank Sinatra's recording of "I Did It My Way."

Moeism:

I never got married. In fact, I went on only three dates. If I'd gotten married, it wouldn't have been fair to a wife because of my life as a golfer. I'd wind up divorced and she'd get everything. I think that's how it works judging by what's happened to friends of mine. I'm very happy being alone.

Moe was a creative artist, equal in talent to musical artists like my brother, Neil, Joni Mitchell, Frank Sinatra (Moe's favorite) and all the other revered artists down through the centuries. That is why Moe's prowess in golf is legendary and on an equal footing with Ben Hogan, Lee Trevino, and the other great ball strikers who will surface as the years roll by. Tiger Woods has been quoted as saying, "Only two people have owned their swing, Ben Hogan and Moe Norman." Tiger says he wants to be the next one. He could be that one. It's obvious to me. Some of what he needs is here and findable in this writing. He has recovered from his car accident and plays golf again.

When I got to know Moe and we became pals, it was interesting watching him come out of his shell of isolation wondering who to trust. He had his doubts, his fears, his fences built, but he survived. He had his goal, and he became the proof that great things are achievable. He had few friends early in life and set up pins in a bowling alley to make a few dollars in the winter. He hit balls all season long at Rockway Golf Club in Kitchener, Ontario, Canada. As the years went by, he became a formidable amateur competitor and amassed an impressive record, but he was an outcast on the amateur circuit.

Moe hitchhiked to tournaments. He slept in bunkers at the tournaments and carried his own bag because he had no money. He hid from the microphones when he won. People did not invite him to their houses. There was a reason for that.

Early in his life, Moe had a serious problem with personal hygiene that had a huge effect on his life for a long time. I remember forty years ago in the early 1980s telling him to wear shirts only once. I recall that because he lived out of his Cadillac with all his clothes on hangars in the back seat.

A Fruit Juice Can

We were going in his car from the New Smyrna Beach municipal course to Wekiva G. C. in the Orlando area. I rolled the window down slightly. Moe was trying, and he thought that if he wore a shirt and sweated into it then let it hang up for a few days that it would be okay. It wasn't. The car was very stuffy. So, I told him, politely, that every time he hit balls and sweated, which for him was a daily occurrence, that whatever he was wearing had to go to the laundry. He followed that advice. It made a big difference. When he met new people, personal hygiene was no longer a problem.

I don't know if this aspect of Moe's life was written about by others who knew him on some basis or knew of him and wrote from that perspective. I saw he was a good guy who was generous with what he could offer to others he liked who tried to play good golf. He ignored those who offended him. When they asked him, "Moe, how do you do that?" He'd say, "Wouldn't you like to know," and walk on.

Moe was a meat and potatoes guy, and some apple pie and ice cream please, and another Coca-Cola. "Yup, that's what I like." The all-you-can-eat buffet style restaurants in Florida and elsewhere were his friends. As the winter months in Florida went by, Moe hit them all and found his favorites. One of them posted a picture of Moe at the entrance and barred him. No entry. He ate too much. The restaurant lost money on Moe.

I remember convincing Moe that his digestive system needed roughage, salads, to offset the lifelong flow of pork chops, pig knuckles, spaghetti and meatballs, roast beef, steaks, and the never ending Coca-Colas that he liked so much. When he was younger, he bought Coca-Cola by the case, twenty-four bottles in a wooden case. I even convinced him to try drinking water. I told him that most of the human body is liquid, water. So, he drank water too and ate salads, minus tomatoes. Our Moe did not like tomatoes.

A Fruit Juice Can

We were walking along one day at Spruce Creek Golf Club near Daytona Beach, Florida, talking about what we were doing and trying to figure out what it meant, where it led. It was a way of life Moe knew well, and he knew that eventually, or in the next heartbeat, life here could end, and the body would go to the cemetery. "Yup," he'd say, "then what?"

So, we talked about that too. We talked about life after death. "There is no death," I told Moe, because that's what I believe. Yes, the body dies and goes back to the Earth, but the soul continues. All of us come to Earth from another location and return to it. Moe wasn't even skeptical about that. He was open.

My brother, Neil, made it possible financially for me to spend all this time with Moe and pursue these things that fascinate me. I always wanted to write and play golf, so I did. I kept notes, writings really, about golf and Moe and other things that are invaluable to what I am trying to convey now to that world out there of golfers and would-be golfers, and others. Much of this writing is about golf, and there is the element about life.

In the winters of the early 1960s, a small army of Canadian golf pros gathered at Tomoka Oaks Golf Course in Ormond Beach, Florida on the north side of Daytona Beach. The objective was to escape from the Canadian winter and learn to hit golf balls and control where they were going. Ball beaters, that's what we were. Every morning, we hit balls on the range, our own balls marked with our individual mark, and then retrieved them and played eighteen holes. Everybody watched Moe. He was so good at it. We lived on nickels and dimes. Tomoka Oaks' owner charged us a dollar a day.

One winter, three of us had a trailer with three beds for one hundred dollars a month total. Golf and housing cost me sixty-three dollars a month. Food was also inexpensive. It was the mid 1960s. We congregated at Mac's Famous Bar, the race car driver's headquarters in those days where films of previous races of the Daytona 500 were shown in the parking lot and where a monster corn beef sandwich was about a dollar. It was also where Mark Hodgson, the brilliant musician, got started in the Daytona area. Draft beer may have been twenty-five cents. The young women of Daytona found us there and in a variety of other Daytona hot spots. "You guys must have left all the ugly ones at home," one of them said to me one day. I guess we looked good, tanned, and in good physical condition. They were definitely on our trail. It was a pleasure to know them.

Moe did not participate in any of this activity. He could be found in the Belair Plaza on the beachside of North Daytona at a bowling alley after his all-you-can-eat buffet meal. The closest Moe ever got to what could be called a date that he told me about was a golf game he played at, I believe, Thornhill G.C., on the north side of Toronto with Marlene Stewart Streit, who is a Canadian women's champion, a member of the Canadian Golf Hall of Fame, The World Golf Hall of Fame, and an Honorary Member of The Royal And Ancient Golf Club Of St. Andrews. Moe remembered that day, fondly. Occasionally, he would mention it to me.

In the mid 1960s, Buffalo Springfield, the band Neil was in, was just beginning to surface on the North American west coast and nationally behind their hit song "For What It's Worth," written by Stephen Stills. They showed up in Florida as opening act for The Beach Boys' North American tour. Neil collapsed on stage from something derivative of grand mal epileptic seizures earlier in his life. I had the same affliction. The energy of a seizure is very, very powerful. It is barely within words to describe the feeling of it. It has always seemed to me that it is an experience that opens a portal to spirituality. There is mysticism involved and a sense of being able to see a far bigger world than most contemplate. The enormity of what is revealed is a life changing experience.

It brought me much closer to energy itself and the desire to create and acquire ever more energy. It also distanced me from any desire to become a proponent of the establishment with its atomic weapons and insane wars. I feel the good energy when I play the piano and guitar, when I write, and when I hit golf balls. A second book I am contemplating, titled, *Cosmic Golf*, will deal with that. I told Moe about this, and he was intrigued. The world of energy drew him in. He knew I was unlike other people he knew.

I saw Moe hit hundreds of thousands of balls when we practiced and played together. We hung out daily, sometimes for months, year after year in Florida and Canada. Moe was an introvert of enormous depth. He was not afraid of winning, but he was uncomfortable with the social aftermath of success, of being a tournament winner, a true champion ball striker, and of dealing with media exposure with the ease of Jack Nicklaus, Lee Trevino, and many others.

He had his own world, a comfort zone mentally, that he protected for self-survival. He didn't want to enter into an arrangement created by someone else that "mixes my life up with yours." He became aware of the effect of how good he was and also aware that he was not sure, confident, of how to deal with being a master striker of the ball and the only one spoken of as an equal to Ben Hogan. Eventually, this led to a schedule of clinics that he really enjoyed. There, he was in control and at ease. He could do things and get a laugh or two. He was a natural ham who now had found his own stage.

Earlier in his life, as an amateur golfer and a human being in our society in Canada in southern Ontario, Moe did not fit in easily, and he did not warrant exclusion. He was not the run of the mill well-groomed amateur player competing in the Ontario Golf Association's summer schedule of tournaments at exclusive private clubs. He was a great ball striker who successfully competed with many excellent players, among them, Phil Brownlee, a member of Canada's Americas Cup team with Gary Cowan, and Nick Weslock, a five-time Canadian Amateur Champion. Gary Cowan won the U.S. Amateur title twice and was another product of the golfing scene in Kitchener / Waterloo, Ontario, Moe's hometown.

Moe won a lot of tournaments and a lot of prizes, including many, many, wrist watches—expensive ones. As an amateur, he was not allowed to make money from golf, but he had no money. However, he had many television sets, and furniture that he won. For a while, he would wear five or six watches, nice ones with gold bands and fancy expensive faces up and down his left or right arm, or both arms. "Want to know what time it is in London, Moscow, Australia?" he'd ask, laughing. Then, one day, the watches would not be there, or not as many of them, but he might have a new pair of shoes, a new pair of pants and shirt. This was noticed.

The deans of amateur golf wondered and saw an opportunity to rid themselves and their golfing events of this social aberration whose golfing talent they admired but who didn't rise to the level of social acceptance that was expected. That Moe could represent Canada seemed to bother them.

The solution was to revoke his amateur status. As the story goes that I was told, officers of the amateur body arrived at Moe's family home in Kitchener and asked to see the prizes he'd won. These were not cops with a search warrant issued by some judge who liked to play golf. They were just self-appointed protectors of the amateur golf rules who, in their eyes, were doing their duty. To them, it was a noble endeavour.

So, they got him. Verdict: guilty. Trial: unnecessary. It was like Alice in Wonderland. In real courts, an often assumption is the accused is guilty unless innocence can be justified. This was not a real court, but what it did affected Moe's life arbitrarily. There is nothing quite like arbitrary power.

Moeism:

I was getting ready to represent Canada in the Americas Cup in Mexico. I had my team jacket, got my inoculations, had my airline tickets. I was excited. I was the Canadian Amateur champion two years running, and I'd be playing against Harvie Ward, the U.S. Amateur Champion two years running. Four days before I was to leave, the Royal Canadian Golf Association convenes a special meeting. From that I received a letter telling me I wasn't a true amateur and please return the jacket and the airline tickets. I returned them. I wasn't an amateur by their definition, and I sure wasn't a pro. Where could I play golf?

Thus, Moe Norman became a professional golfer, a famous one to this day. Now, he was "allowed" to make money from golf. So, he did, and whatever he made he carried in his pocket as an ever-increasing wad of financial power. Banks? No, it stayed in the pocket where he had instant access. Eventually, he used banks, but he never put all his money in them. When he died, about $30,000 was found hidden in the trunk of his car and in various other places. He had a huge cardboard box full of golf balls in the trunk where he kept some of it.

It's nice to make note that the church was full of people at his funeral service.

CHAPTER 2
PINE VALLEY

"Where's the driver from this set of Hogan woods?" George Clifton looked around his pro shop at Pine Valley Golf Club in Woodbridge, Ontario, in Canada. Bob Breen, the first assistant didn't know. I didn't either.

Fergie (John Ferguson), who ran the back shop, had no idea. Pine Valley had a civilized membership, so we weren't expecting a theft, but where was that Hogan driver, a fine persimmon wood design approved by Ben himself? This was in 1963 or thereabouts. It wasn't a particularly busy day, not a lot of play. Where was that driver? How long had it been missing? Who had been in and out of the pro shop?

Finally, I remembered that Moe Norman had been in the shop prowling around looking at this club and that and humming/singing "Row, row, row your boat gently down the stream...life is but a dream." George walked out to the first tee, which was right outside the pro shop. He scanned the first hole. No Moe. Then, in the distance, a lone player and the trademark swing: a dead giveaway.

"Was Moe looking at that driver?"

"Probably, he was here looking at this and that," I said.

"He's probably got it," said George.

A while later, Moe showed up. Sure enough, he had the Hogan driver.

"Nice, yup, nice feel, George. I like it." George looked at the face of the club.

No marks on it. He put it back on the rack. Mystery solved.

Pine Valley Golf Club is now The National Club, but back in the day, when Woodbridge, Ontario was "dry"—that is, dry of alcohol and a possible descendant of The Women's Christian Temperance Union, the custodian of Pine Valley— its owner, Jack Bailey, had a different view of civilized hospitality. Thus, the establishment operated wide open. Now, about fifty-five years later, it is doubtful that full exposure of the blatant flouting of the law banning the alcohol trade at the social level at Pine Valley Golf Club in Vaughan Township would matter to anyone. There's no one left alive to get even with, to prosecute and fine.

The memory of the good times there remains to this day, the music blasting, people dancing, the beer and wine and a variety of liquors flowing freely. Now, in Ontario, it is legal to smoke marijuana anywhere that it's legal to smoke tobacco, so I can say that the atmosphere would have included the smoke of the finest marijuana of the day. There was no closing time. Leonard Cohen had not written the song "Closing Time" yet. It came later, a truly great song.

One of the frequent "guest" members at Pine Valley was a sitting member of the LCBO, the Liquor Control Board of Ontario, the licensing entity for the province. Sometimes the weekend partying raved on until the wee hours.

The cops played golf at Pine Valley as guests and took care of all minor irritants like speeding and parking tickets. All the major bookies played golf there, as did the real estate land developers and construction kings of the day. Added to that, coming and going regularly were members of the Toronto Argonaut football team and players from the Toronto Maple Leaf hockey team, most of whom I'd already met from attending the home games at Maple Leaf Gardens.

The Leaf coach, Punch Imlach, and my father, Scott Young, were good friends. My father was the Toronto *Globe and Mail* sports columnist and had hosted

Hockey Night in Canada's intermission, between-period nationally televised interviews. He was very well-known nationally. I had access to the press room and the Maple Leaf team dressing room when I was a kid. I played junior tournament golf in the summer and hockey in winter in Ontario as captain of a team that made it to the provincial finals. That was the "normal" of my existence.

Pine Valley Golf Club had, in a word, "protection"; civilized, informal protection against interference with its lifestyle, a lifestyle that was essentially harmless and enjoyable and never dangerous. Moe Norman was part of the scenery of the day. He did not attend the social gatherings. He drank only Coca-Cola and no coffee or tea. Our Moe was a conscientious athlete.

I had been one of the better amateurs in Ontario's provincial golf tournament circuit, and at Pine Valley, Moe and I got to know each other better as golfers. I always liked him and admired his prowess as a ball striker. As human beings go, Moe was an unusual specimen.

One peaceful Monday morning about 7:30 a.m., a police flotilla of several cars arrived. It had been a particularly raucous weekend but, as I said, we of Pine Valley had "protection." So, the raid was low key. They showed up when no one was there and not in the middle of the previous evening's festivities, when they would have run the risk of arresting many, many people, several of whom would likely be publicly known. The national news media would have had a field day. The parking lot was empty. Not one golfer was on the course. The clubhouse wasn't open yet. No one was there except Fergie, me, and Jack Bailey, the club owner, who was asleep in his office.

Fergie ran the back shop and took care of the member's clubs. We were sitting in front of the pro shop with our morning coffee, planning our break and entry to the clubhouse kitchen to filch our breakfast. We heard a rumble of cars coming in from Pine Valley Drive up the gravel road hill. It was over a quarter of a mile, then they entered the parking lot. We could see them across the first tee and the eighth fairway. All the cars were the same, government green.

"Cops!" said Fergie.

I headed immediately to the clubhouse front door with my nail file in hand, which was all that I needed to pick the lock. I knew that Jack Bailey was asleep in his office. At some point the previous night, we had been standing on the bar singing. I could see Jack's Lincoln in a small parking lot hidden by bushes behind the clubhouse.

"Get up, Jack," I said. "The cops are here. You got to go out the office window to your car and go out the back way down the eighteenth fairway to that trail and get out of here." It was a rude awakening, but he moved fast, hangover and all. I went back out the front door of the clubhouse as the cops arrived.

These were not the cops who played golf, but they were polite. They also looked like they wished they were somewhere else. As I walked back to the pro shop, I glimpsed Jack's Lincoln slinking past a fairway bunker on the eighteenth hole. His escape was successful.

"Is the manager here?" the head cop asked.

"No, not yet," I told him, "but I can call him." The manager was new, just at the club for a few days, maybe a week. The pro shop staff, Bob Breen, me, and Fergie, had already had one run in with him. I can't remember his name. First impressions were not good. He came to the pro shop door a day or two after his arrival and asked if anyone from the pro shop had been in the club house kitchen because something was missing. Bob Breen wasn't at work yet, so I told him that I couldn't tell him who had been there.

We ate in the clubhouse daily. Sometimes Moe ate there too. The food at Pine Valley was good. When it was early before the kitchen staff arrived and we needed food, we got it ourselves. When Bob Breen arrived later in the morning, it surfaced that he had taken two slices of bread and made a sandwich. He was hungry. The new manager saw this as theft, breaking and entering, and so on. We thought he was a crazed asshole. He banned us from the clubhouse. Really. When George Clifton arrived and heard the story, he closed the pro shop for dinner and ordered food from a nearby restaurant in Woodbridge.

We set up a table with candles and were eating dinner when Jack Bailey arrived at the pro shop door. He had been somewhere else and arrived to find the pro shop closed for the dinner hour. He was amused but didn't know what had happened. George explained it. Peace ensued. Jack brokered a deal that resurrected normalcy, but the bad vibe continued.

The new manager didn't like us being in the club house socializing with the members. Protocol was being breached, but this was Pine Valley, not some formal, some would say, snooty, upper class private club that I had been used to as a junior golfer in Ontario, and I do not mean Summit Golf Club in Richmond Hill, Ontario where I had been a junior member. Summit was comfortable.

So, there I was with this quiet police officer at 8:00 a.m. Police do understand alcohol. They are familiar with it, personally and professionally. I located the manager. It was a while before he arrived. The police entered the clubhouse and began unloading beer cases and liquor and wine bottles and putting them in a truck. There was not one full bottle of anything left. The police were seizing empty bottles. The new manager arrived as the seizures ended. He was arrested, and they all left. Jack Bailey called later in the morning and I told him what happened. I guess he posted bail. I don't remember. Fergie thought justice had prevailed. Life at Happy Knoll.

It was an interesting start to the week. The complainants perhaps thought they had struck a blow for right thinking people, those of moderation in all things. Thus, their desire to center out the heathens who used alcohol as fuel for a variety of unseemly transgressions was dutifully served, but briefly, very briefly. Things were back together within a few days. The booze was stashed in individual member's lockers, the wine and liquor that is, and beer was brought in and the empties removed regularly. The party raved on, mildly subdued. It was good at Pine Valley.

In Moe's daily world in those days, he went to De Haviland driving range, his professional affiliation, and hit balls, or didn't, and wandered away and got in his car and drifted around from golf course to golf course seeing people he knew, playing a few holes here and there, using the putting greens, and drinking Coca-Colas. He carried all his money in his pocket. Banks were in his future.

It was decades before he became interested in giving clinics and getting paid. He was a natural "ham." He liked playing to the assembled gathering. It was good to watch. Good entertainment. David Feherty of the Golf Channel would have liked that part of Moe; he always struck me as a would-be Broadway actor who lost his way to New York and found himself at a golf course. Now, he stars on national golf broadcasts, but he's still on the way to Broadway.

That was how I got to know Moe better. I knew him from playing amateur golf tournaments in Ontario when I was a kid. Moe was about twelve years older than me. He came by Pine Valley frequently. He knew me previously as one of the five or six best amateurs in the province of Ontario, as someone who was trying to play good golf. He understood that.

He was a lonely figure, socially inept but not unfriendly. He was an offbeat character and an occasional subject of my father's sports column in the Toronto *Globe and Mail*. His prowess as a ball striker was growing.

George Clifton owned a camera that would shoot at 1/1000th of a second shutter speed. It was a military grade the Air Force used. George photographed Moe so we had long spools of pictures of Moe's swing showing all the positions he hit. Graves Golf Academy has none of those yet, but they are looking.

Moe was very strong, physically. He hit thousands of balls from one end of the bag of clubs to the other. He liked practicing with a driver. "Everything else is within that," he said. He also hit many, many, four-wood shots so the full swing was also hitting balls off the ground, and that was important.

Moe knew only golf early in life. It expanded as the years rolled by. Funny things happened along the way. There was the traffic stop in Alberta where he pulled a wad of $15,000 to $20,000 from his pocket thinking that the fine could be paid on the spot. The cop was slack-jawed by that one. And then there was the unforgettable dinner in Victoria, British Columbia.

We were there to play the British Columbia Provincial Open championship. The dinner had been arranged by Bill Wakeham, a B.C. Open champion. We were on the road playing an early version of the Canadian Tour, an organized schedule of provincial Opens plus some other tournaments. It was a beginning. We were playing for nickels and dimes.

Moe was seated across the table from me. There was a woman on each side of him. I looked the situation over. Eight or ten people were at the table. Bill Wakeham, also known as "the Chopper," was at the head of the table. I caught his eye. He smiled. He had probably arranged the seating on purpose. Moe was definitely out of his league. He didn't know what to say or do.

Alvie Thompson, "the Stinger," was on my left. He had won the CPGA Championship in a playoff with George Knudson and Stan Leonard by shooting 63 in a playoff at Mississauga Golf Club near Toronto. He was a great friend and the best putter Moe or I ever knew. I'll reveal his methodology later in this writing. He also knew Moe well. All the players did. Moe tried, and I tried to help him in the dinner table banter.

Appetizers were served and time passed, too much time for Moe. He was hungry. He wanted to eat and get out of the situation he was in.

"I don't know anything except golf," he finally told the two women in response to their attempt to communicate with him. They smiled and they were polite. Gradually, they were figuring out that Moe was unusual. They thought he was just shy. They were right about that. Alvie and I were watching this drama unfold in front of us.

The appetizers were served and eaten. Moe didn't like appetizers. He wanted pork chops, vegetables, and mashed potatoes, and another Coke please. The appetizers took about forty-five minutes. Moe was hungry and trapped. It ended on an unusual note from Moe. In a fit of exasperation and hunger, out it came, loudly.

"Where the fuck is the food?" He was serious.

We were laughing. Moe never said anything like that. The food arrived quickly, and all was well. The story of the "where the fuck is the food" dinner is fondly remembered. It was about fifty-five years ago.

There are many "Moeisms." Those who got to know him well, people in the golf business, have stories. I have too. Some I will probably never divulge and others I will.

CHAPTER 3
A BALL STRIKER

Moe Norman's prowess as a ball striker is recognized throughout golfdom. Moe's system of mechanics is simple, and his description of it is excellent. Gary Player said in my presence one day in Florida that Moe was a great teacher for good players. Lee Trevino said in the late 1980s that Moe could have won any major and still could. Moe was fifty-nine or sixty years old then.

A study of what Moe was doing in the realm of mechanics lead inevitably to the question of the mental action that recreates excellence shot after shot after shot, day after day after day, year after year after year. What causes that? It is the only relevant question when the perfect shot is struck. What indeed causes that? The answer to that question draws like a magnet those little gems of insight, which, in commercial parlance can be termed, "golf oil." When I asked Moe questions about those mind-driven things that make it all work right, those little gems of "golf oil" oozed out of the old Moeski, and I flowed with it. But more about "golf oil" later.

In the winter of the late 1970s and early 1980s, Moe and I played nine holes most afternoons at Spruce Creek Golf Club near Daytona Beach, FL. Preceding this, we would meet in the mornings and hit 250 to 300 balls each. We hit three or four balls a hole off the tee and innumerable chip shots and putts on each hole. The ninth hole then (maybe now the eighteenth) was a dogleg-left par four.

For several days, we had been talking about figuring out how to try to hit the ball into the hole from the fairway. This stemmed from discussions about putting. It was obvious to me that it was fundamental to create a clear image of the ball going into the hole, and that is what I was trying to do. To simplify it, I envisioned the ball landing in the hole on the fly whenever possible, as opposed to seeing it land and roll into the hole. It was from this exercise and by realizing the significance of being able to locate and establish the apex of the ball's flight that I began to develop the terminology to describe the technique of assembling the image of the *shot-to-be*.

On the ninth hole one day, I saw the flight of the ball into the hole as one complete image that included the physical motion of the swing. It lit up in my mind's eye in pristine clarity, and I felt it physically. I'll never forget it. The ball, in fact, landed in the hole. When it was in the air, I said something to Moe like "that could go in."

From his perspective, I'd been trying to convince him that it must be possible to understand what happens to cause the ball to go into the hole, then, it happened. It was a full seven-iron shot.

It has taken a long time to develop a coherent way to set out this technique. Recently, because I am focused on these writings, I've gained insights as to how to refine the technique. Now, I'd like to hit a few hundred balls each day and play golf just to see what I can let happen.

My guess is that those who played golf with Ben Hogan noticed a difference in the flight of his shots. The same is true of Moe Norman. Where there is a sophisticated degree of directness to the hit that is consistently centered properly, the parameters of the equation of ball striking are elevated and freed so that direct mental control is enhanced. This only creates more freedom and ease. *The sound of the shot thickens, almost as though it is wet.*

Mind Golf is about how to gain that freedom and ease. It is the quest of many besides me. There is no end to this quest that I can see. The more accurate I get, the farther the ball flies. Mind power, itself, has the attribute of relentless expansion and increase. Everyone has a mind to use. You might as well aim at perfection. What could be the alternative, if not unsatisfying mediocrity? It is possible to achieve a mental state that allows the conscious acquisition of more energy, then use it to deliver the golf ball ever-increasing distances with absolute accuracy.

In the text of this book, there is mention of a field in Oak Hill, Florida where Moe and I hit a lot of balls in the accompaniment of six very large Brahman cattle. It is true that a lot happened in that field that was important to the art of ball striking. To me, the most significant thing happened one morning when Moe said, "You're getting the ball in the air faster than me." That meant I had the club face on the ball slightly longer than Moe. My accuracy was absolute. Then he said, "You are the closest in the game to Hogan."

That stopped me. I hadn't thought of it that way, but my ball striking ability was extremely good and improving. Pureness of technique was a given. Moe was watching with interest. We had been hitting balls for years and playing golf for decades. I didn't write about this until now because I realize the magnitude of the claim, "the closest in the game to Ben Hogan." Really? But it was Moe who said that, and that gives it a flavor that is authentic, because he knew whereof he spoke.

My swing was free, mentally created, and my body had the feeling of the shot-to-be. It was easy and effortless. It would be pleasant to do that again.

As this unfolded, I became aware of greater possibilities. The major one was increased achievable distance with a driver. One day I noticed that by "seeing," that is, forming the image of the shot-to-be, that I could regulate the distance the ball traveled mentally, through the creation of the image itself. No additional physical power was required.

That was my initial perception, and I took that idea to hitting a lot of tee shots daily. I looked at my longest drives, and each day, I increased the mental image by about three to five feet. I kept doing that, and each day, I added another three to five feet. The average distance began to appear to me to be increasing.

In a month, it was obvious it was working. My average distance increased by about fifteen yards without increased physical effort. If anything, it was easier, physically. I knew I was on to something significant. On the course, I was closer to the greens by a club, sometimes more. I was very accurate.

One afternoon at Spruce Creek Golf Club, I hit the pin four times in nine holes and shot 30, six under par. Moe was impressed. It was fascinating, and easy. More distance off the tee was what I needed. Now better putting was required to bring me to a new level. Eventually, the mental technique of creating the image of the shot-to-be was portable to putting. It took time and a highly refined putting grip to figure that out.

The revelations in the field in Oak Hill and the New Smyrna Beach sports area took place in the early 1980s. Now, my grasp of what happened and how to communicate it is far more advanced. In a nutshell, it is based on the acquisition of more mental energy and using it to create the image of the desired shot-to-be, the right shot.

In all the publicity about Moe in the 1990s around the Titleist Company's wonderful gesture of guaranteeing him $5,000 each month for life and, the commercial items put out by Natural Golf that are instruction related, there is very little mention of the things he told me and showed me, and virtually no mention of the things he and I discussed regarding the mental aspect of striking the ball. It is that which is the subject of much of this dissertation.

Here is a perfect example of what is meant by that:

February 12, 2003, approximately a year prior to Moe's passing. Location: New Smyrna Beach Golf Club, Florida.

Moe and I have been meeting here most mornings and spending an hour to an hour and a half on the putting green, talking and putting. It has been very productive for both of us. I've explained to Moe a refinement in the mental side of the putting technique coupled with an alteration in the grip and the mechanics of the stroke. He has adopted those suggestions. They will be explained in some detail later.

When what I've suggested is accomplished, the ball goes to the hole. It doesn't always go into the hole, but it wants to, and were it not for footprints and other alterations because of human traffic, the increase in holed putts would be higher.

Today we're going to the practice range. Moe has bought a pail of balls. He never does that. The people on the range retreat a respectful distance when they see Moe and me coming and watch. Today he wants to show me the result of the suggestion I made to him a few days ago that he balance himself for the end of the roll-line of the putt and, as well, balance himself in the *ready position* for the *apex-fall line* of full shots. We'll talk more about the ready position and the apex-fall line later.

For the past several days, he has been doing that in his daily nine-hole round at Royal Oak Golf Course in Titusville, Florida, where he plays three or four balls a hole. He wants to show me what he can now accomplish.

"My balance is better than ever," he says. Then he shows me. It is a masterful exhibition of ball striking. "It has never been easier for me; no stress, no tension, I'm as loose as a goose. All my life," he says, "wrong." That stops me. A few moments of silence pass.

"No, you aren't wrong," I say. "You just never thought of it this way; neither did I. It makes it easier for you."

Usually, Moe would hit straight shots. Today, he is hitting high and low fades and draws with any club he chooses and enjoying it. His normal wide stance is closer to conventional. I have never seen him do that in all the hundreds of thousands of balls he and I hit in practice.

In his round the day before, he had hit several shots and felt the initial vibration in the shaft when the face of the club touched the ball. He was impressed. It came at the end of his career and was a huge step that elevated the excellence for which he was so famous. Very few saw what I saw that day. It was the gem of polished excellence.

Nota Bene (The next several pages outline a legal matter that is relevant to my professional golfing relationship with Moe Norman despite the fact it has nothing to do with golf):

You might wonder why I never competed professionally and showed what I was capable of doing. The level of expertise I achieved in that field in Oak Hill, Florida was never exhibited in week to week competition because of what became a multiyear legal proceeding in Toronto, Ontario, Canada, wherein I was one of twelve defendants in a massive marijuana and hashish conspiracy trial. It was Canada's "flagship" soft drug case, Regina vs Rowbotham et al. The federal government's police and lawyers would show the tax paying public how efficient, thoughtful, and protective they were. In fact, they were inefficient, illegally devious, and destructive.

The day I left for Toronto, I met Moe in that field and picked out my nine iron. About 125 yards away was a tree that was five or six inches across. I hit the trunk four times in a row dead center and that was it. I said goodbye to Moe and drove away. I'll never forget the look on his face. As the years went by, he was always there for me, helping financially, as was my brother, and picking me up to play golf when I didn't have a car.

Canada's flagship soft drug trial became a corrupt prosecution. Actually, it wasn't a prosecution, it was a persecution conducted by those entrusted with the public trust. The deans of the administration of justice of the day were determined to get us. The current "deans" have a wonderful opportunity now to right a monumental wrong. The trial led to convictions that were overturned on appeal principally because of the "plain view" offence in open court of jury tampering and obstruction of justice committed by the trial judge, Eugene Ewaschuk, who, in my view was, and maybe still is, a right wing cowboy and a very strange human being.

The jury selection process of the day allowed the prosecution four peremptory challenges and forty-eight "stand-asides." The stand-asides sat together to be reconsidered when a panel of prospective jurors was exhausted and prior to another panel being called. Until he broke the law, Ewaschuk adhered to that lawful process designed and made law by the Parliament of Canada. Thus, the stand-asides were a collection of prosecution undesirables numbering about twenty-five with three or four empty seats to fill in the jury box, and the current panel was down to zero. The prosecutor had neither peremptory challenges nor stand-asides left.

Ewaschuk looked them over and, with the mind of a crown prosecutor, found them to be an unsavoury crew. He had also met with prosecution representatives prior to the trial and understood their position. The prosecution could lose with those people in the jury. His solution was simple but not simple minded. It was predatory and illegal. He called another panel, thus illegally creating an additional twenty-five or more peremptory challenges for the prosecutor, Christopher Amerasinghe. Amerasinghe, the people's advocate for truth and justice, did not complain.

Ewaschuk decided alone that the Parliament of Canada's lawful process of selecting jury members was sadly lacking, and like a pioneer, he decided to redesign it. "Tex," as he is known, thus struck a blow for judges who don't like juries that interfere with their point of view. He also broke the law and shattered the legal process that casts in stone a defendant's right to a jury of peers. In

Tex Ewaschuk's eyes, mind, and blood, all were guilty and no jury was going to be allowed to change that under his watch if he could arrange it. He did his best, and his approach carried over into other cases. Unfortunately, he was supported in this transgression by none other than the Chief Justice of the Supreme Court of Ontario's Trial Division, Justice Gregory Evans. This act created a conspiracy of jury tampering, obstruction of justice, and conspiracy to subvert the administration of justice. In addition, the desired objectives of the conspiracy were achieved. The damage of illegal imprisonment was successful. It was severe and long lasting. Many subsequent Ewaschuk "trials" were overturned on appeal because of jury related transgressions and at what cost to the downtrodden taxpaying public? Ewaschuk instigated what Leonard Cohen, the revered writer of many works of art, so wisely advised against when he wrote not to "ka-ka" in your uniform.

Neither Tex Ewaschuk nor Gregory Evans were charged. Why? The answer to that will be very revealing. When I testified, Ewaschuk had a pistol on his desk that was out of sight of the others in the courtroom. He wanted me to see it. He liked that idea. It suited his grasp of impartiality. It had what appeared to be a pearl handle but was probably plastic like something from a Roy Rogers movie or the television series of yesteryear, *Gunsmoke*. Are you supposed to love your judge?

That trial spanned about thirteen months, and its descendants went on for another seven or eight years. It began in 1982. It was 1992 before I was free of it. However, it lingers on and has contributed to health problems including high blood pressure, impaired vision, and an irregular heart beat due to ongoing stress which, in my view, is derivative of my hesitancy in going to the national news media and energetically exposing the illegality of the subversion of the jury selection process committed by Ewaschuk and the complicity in that act of the administration of justice of the day. I should have done that. Also present were the many "officers of the court," all of whom are culpable, that is, defence and prosecution lawyers and the key police officers. Several of the defence lawyers are now judges, and, from what I hear, good judges, but they were trapped with the quiet threat of career destruction through adverse rulings in other cases if they did not comply with the obstructionist and blatantly illegal modus operandi of the hierarchy of the administration of justice of the day. In joining with the subversion of the administration of justice, regardless of the reason, they became, and are to this day, complicit and culpable. Their rescue should begin with an admission of the truth and a public effort to right the wrong that has been studiously buried by the current administration of justice and its predecessors. There are obviously similar cases now and over the past three and a half decades. Defence counsel are silent on this for the obvious reason that it is an ongoing practice of predatory, authoritarian, and dictatorial theft of the public trust that is out of sight and yet, in plain view. In this created reality, the law of man has become the law of men. "Trials" with a jury of peers are embroidery, camouflage, over what has already been decided when individuals decide that a finding of guilt will be the outcome.

There is much more to this and it will be exposed. There is no statute of limitations to hide behind, and marijuana is now legal in Canada. Publicity and a civil action will likely initiate the exposure.

It will be educational to watch the current administration of justice wrestle with this, given its silence for thirty-seven years, and with the separate matter of charging Eugene Ewaschuk and bringing him to trial in a criminal proceeding that could lead to a lengthy prison sentence. "Tex" will wonder about his future. I don't know his age. In April of 2022, I became eighty years of age.

Justice delayed, as the saying goes, is justice denied.

My title for this sordid denigration of the sacrosanct status of justice in our society is this: JUSTICE MOST FOUL.

It deserves a documentary production for the Toronto International Film Festival that qualifies for acceptance in the international film festival circuit. If it were ever made, I would cooperate with the production of that film. My brother, Neil, suggested I do that. I like the idea. It can happen.

Moe was a stalwart friend in life. He helped me when I needed help and I helped him. We talked about golf, and he read the notes and writings I accumulated.

"Nobody knows what you know," he would say from time to time.

I think others including Moe knew what I was trying to articulate but didn't know how to express it in any detail. "Visualize the shot," was about as far as it got. Tom Watson mentioned that he wanted the whole body to feel the whole shot. It's a good feeling. Lots of good players have felt it. It comes and goes.

Give that feeling a home within your mind, your life. It is good to have a quiet mind, very quiet. A quiet mind is peaceful and receptive. It is an excellent base for creativity. In golf, the next shot is an artistic creation. The quiet mind commands, and yet, it obeys; it creates and empowers the manifestation of the shot-to-be. Moe revered the quiet mind. He avoided circumstance and people that intruded on the quietness he held dear.

When Moe said, "It's like music," he meant, *the creation of music*. That quiet state of mind does bring the creation of music, the writing of songs. The "whoosh" of the physical motion of the golf swing and the "crack" at impact when the club touches and holds the ball momentarily comprises the sound of the music of the song; the lyrical content is expressed as the flight of the shot-that-is. It is the manifestation of the power in the creation of the original thought-form of the flight of the shot-to-be.

I tested what I learned in that field in Oak Hill in a tournament in St. Augustine, Florida before I left for Canada. I hit sixteen greens in one round and seventeen in the other. It was easy. Good putting would have put me far under par. One of my fellow competitors made a point of telling me what a great swing I had. I mentioned Moe Norman, and he was awestruck.

CHAPTER 4
IT'S LIKE MUSIC

I met Moe when I was eighteen, playing amateur golf in the province of Ontario in Canada. We played a lot of golf together over the years from the early 1960s in friendly games and on the original version of the Canadian Tour, and in events staged by the North Florida PGA. In one span of five years in the late 1970s and early 1980s, we hit hundreds of balls each morning all winter long for six months in Florida, then chipped and putted for a couple of hours in the early afternoon, and finished the golfing day off by playing nine holes with three or four balls a hole. It was a perfect way to practice and learn, and we continued this in Canada.

Occasionally, someone from the PGA Tour would come by and hit balls with us. Not many knew where to find us, but Wally Kuchar, Matt Kuchar's uncle, was one who came by from time to time. Wally was a good player. I believe he finished fourth at Doral on the PGA Tour one year in the early 1980s or late '70s. It was Wally who was present one day when the significance of the apex of the ball's flight was becoming apparent to me. We discussed it. I was hitting identical shots with a two-and-a-half wood persimmon club. The target was a purple weed about 235 yards away. I was trying to cause the ball to fall on the weed, and I wasn't missing it by much. Wally told me once that when he visited Moe and me, he made notes when he went home about what we discussed. Now I should see if he still has those notes or find out if his nephew, Matt Kuchar, the very successful PGA Tour player, knows of them.

I am in New Smyrna Beach culling from my notes of thirty-five or forty years what will be in this book and adding to what already exists as I proceed. I am getting new shafts for my clubs; shafts with more flex, because I am not as strong as I used to be.

I am thinking about and noticing the similarities in golf and music. The guitar is my new driver, my nine iron, or whichever club I pull from the bag. The sound I cause the guitar to produce is the counterpart of the physical motion that produces the desired flight of the ball.

It's really a state of mind that is portable from one endeavor to another. I want to play the guitar more and hit more golf balls, so I am doing both. I know how to tune to the state of mind that causes the ball to go to the destination point of choice along the flight path I create. That state of mind is portable to creating the sound of the guitar and vocal as one thing; the creative spark that wrote the lyric sets the stage for the meaning of the lyric to drive the action. That way, it sounds sincere, and it is; people like it, but it is not easy to do if you have never done it before. Golf and ball striking are not easy either, but it's worth the effort.

My brother, Neil Young, the acclaimed singer-songwriter, knows how to walk on to a stage and do what I just described. I can see how that works, but I've never done it. The technique of guitar playing, and song writing and singing, requires a degree of expertise that is comparable to assembling the image of the shot-to-be and being able to deliver the swing motion that produces the desired flight of the ball.

Alone, I get better and better playing a guitar, just like hitting balls makes you more familiar with how it really works *if the correct concept is practiced.* I hit the ball because I like to watch it go where I want it to go the way I want it to get there. The same thing is possible for a singer-songwriter with his or her instrument of choice.

Moe Norman used to say occasionally, "It's like music." He meant hitting balls, thousands of them. It's another world, a haven. It is peaceful. He also said, "you have to love your clubs." At night, wherever he was, he took his clubs from the trunk of his car to his bedroom. The average golfer is not likely going to do that, but some kid who gets dedicated and dreams of playing the PGA Tour may very well do that.

Over the years, Moe made many comments about the average golfer, little gems that stuck in my mind for all these years. "They're ball bound," was one of his observations. He meant the focus of attention was on the ball rather than the shot, the flight of the ball, and the feel of the shot itself. Moe's mechanics were, and are, simple. It's *feel*, he would say, for what you want to see that makes it work. "You and I know, Bob," he said one day, "but the members don't know." He meant the members of all golf clubs worldwide.

Moe and Me

Moe and I talked a lot about energy and where it comes from and how to get more of it. Some of what follows is a sample of the kind of discussion I instigated that fascinated Moe. At first, it appears to have nothing to do with golf, then it does, and it has a lot to do with life. Moe was into it. He wanted more. Once, he looked at me in the midst of one of these energy-related discussions and said, "Don't leave me in life."

"Moe," I said one day by the New Smyrna airport when we were practicing. "Do you know that in physics everything that exists has an atomic presence, and spins, revolves? "

He said nothing, but he was listening.

"Think of it this way, the planets in our solar system revolve around the Sun, so there is an obvious connection between the Sun and each planet, something like a line of power, of energy, that maintains the orbit of the Earth around the Sun."

I can tell he was wondering where this was going, but he was intrigued, listening.

"We know energy exists because we feel it and we have the conscious power to use it. So, the Sun supplies energy, lots of it, and its connection to the Earth is probably at the Earth's center. If we consciously establish a connection mentally to the Earth's center, we can tap that flow of energy and increase the flow of energy we have available, because we are already connected to it even if we don't know it and think of it that way."

"Is that what you're doing?"

"I think I'm doing that," I answered. "That's what I'm doing when I tell you I feel lighter on my feet and the colors around me are brighter. That's when I see the line of energy where the air glows or looks hot, in the flight line of the shot I want to hit. "

"Yeah," he says. "You showed me that. You showed me that light."

We had discussed this before, and now he sees the air change too. A mutual friend, Alvie Thompson, a CPGA (Canadian Professional Golfers Association) champion and the best putter Moe and I ever knew, told me one day in the mid 1960s, when I asked him if he saw the grass change color on the line of a putt, "You have to figure that one out yourself." But he acknowledged it happened and didn't know how to explain why. It was about fifteen years before I really started to delve into these ideas. Now, I know it is real. Moe and I were on the case, daily.

"Our Sun keeps us alive, Moe. Every solar system has a Sun, and wherever the center of the universe is, there has to be a Great Central Sun around which all solar systems revolve or, and this is what I believe, within which they all exist." Interesting, and related to acquiring more energy by tuning mentally to the Earth's center was something that Moe thought could be imagined when I suggested it to him.

I told Moe that I felt it eased everything to be able to do this. It helped my efforts to tune to what is called the *etheric body, the body that moves with ease*, which was another topic of discussion we had in the early 1980s and I practice daily.

The etheric body is the exact duplicate of the physical body. Imagine a being within your skin that you can feel which occupies the same feet, legs, torso, neck, head, brain structure, and senses of touch, taste, smell, hearing, eyesight, and consciousness. I call the etheric body "it." When "it" breathes out, the physical body breathes in, and as the physical exhales, the etheric body breathes in. The consciousness of the etheric body lives in a very large world, in universality, with access to that energy. Tune to the Earth's center through the etheric body.

It sounds easy, but it took me some time to do this. However, it's worth the effort. Let "it," the etheric body, do whatever it is you are doing, whether it is hitting golf balls and forming the image of the *shot-to-be* or playing the guitar or painting pictures.

I think artists of all genres and athletes slip into this frame of mind naturally from time to time when they are focused on what they are doing. It comes and goes. My intention was, and is, to develop the technique of recreating that mind set and using it to accomplish whatever it is I am doing. Tuning to the etheric body is the objective. It takes practice.

Playing golf is an act of personal creation. Each shot is an individual creative act, as is the overall approach to playing an eighteen-hole round, or a series of them, especially in competition. Anyone attracted to the mysteries of the power in the creation of thought should look at the game of golf. The art of playing the great game allows the player to practice and gain knowledge of personal use of the power in the creation of thought. Consciousness, vision, action—a melding of mind and body—is the name of the game.

This book is about learning how to strike the golf ball. On the physical side of the equation, it is a description of the mechanics of making direct contact between the ball and the "sweet spot" of the club face and delivering a direct hit; on the mental side, it is the description of a technique for assembling the image for the *shot-to-be* and triggering the feel for a direct hit. In itself, it is an exercise in mind control and a refined technique of visualization. It has to do with personal control of the power in the creation of thought. The physical motion is the result of the creation of the mental construct. The two cannot be separated.

CHAPTER 5
THE CHOSEN LINE

CREATION OF THE SHOT-THAT-IS:

One day on the practice area we had in the late 1970s in New Smyrna Beach, Florida, I looked at Moe and said, "What's in your mind before you hit the ball? What do you do mentally to set up the shot?"

There was a long and thoughtful pause, then he looked at me very intently, as if trying to convey telepathically the meaning of these words. He said: "You have to make the chosen line of aim." He was emphatic. A plane coasted by and landed at the New Smyrna Beach airport. It was an omen. *Making*, that is, constructing, *the chosen line of aim* is an art in itself. I figured out how to do that, and when I showed Moe, he got better instantly in that it made it much easier for him to execute the chosen shot.

Moe played quickly on the course. On the practice fairway, he hit balls the same way. He executed the swing as he *created the shot-to-be* that immediately became *the shot-that-is*. It took a very few seconds. He hit putts the same way. To the observer, he never lined up the putts but, in his mind, he did. And he did exactly the same thing in competition.

I watched this happen without knowing at first the mental depth it involved. Now I know that this is the key to solving ball striking. Moe owned his swing. Tiger Woods saw that and said so. He'd like to do the same thing now. Maybe Tiger will read this book about Moe and me and get something useful from it. I think he would. I know more, however, than I can write. It takes personal contact to say the right thing at the right moment to anyone trying to learn what makes it work.

Moe understood exactly what made it work. He knew it was all mentally driven, conceived, and manifested, but he didn't know how to describe it in any detail. "You have to make the chosen line of aim" was as far as it got, but it implied something more than the admonition to visualize the shot.

He saw an image of a set of railway tracks off into the distance as a way of moving so that the club face was delivered, released, down "the chosen line of aim." He did that early in his life and still used it.

The word "make" made a difference, and the more I thought about it, the more I thought about it. Eventually, I figured it out, and what I figured out is in this writing, and Moe agreed with it and used it.

Mind Golf

On the golf course, Moe looked at the shot, instantly knew the right shot for him, and hit the ball. "The first impression is the one to go with," he told me. He looked at the shot briefly with his left hand on the grip, then set his grip and extended his left arm to place the club face behind the ball.

Simultaneously, he established his balance and put his right hand on the grip. At the same time, his eyes had another look at the shot, and his right foot set. Often, he adjusted the position of the toe of his right shoe as the club head was placed several inches behind the ball into the beginning of the takeaway, the first part of the backswing.

The "ready position" was thus established, with his legs ready for the reversal, the moment the backswing would change direction to become the downswing; then the swing motion started. His weight immediately went to his right heel and his legs were simultaneously moving into the reversal position. In the reversal, Moe's knees bent.

At address, in the "ready position" his legs were straight, but his knees were not locked, and his stance was wider than most players. It was the position his legs adopted in the reversal that was similar to the act of beginning to sit down that allowed him to maintain a "single plane" action and have the club face go directly down "the chosen line of aim" of the shot-to-be as far as his arms could comfortably extend.

In the absence of being able to watch Moe in person, it's necessary to watch video and film of this to get it, to get a clue as to how to understand how it works. "It's so simple," as Moe so often said. Check out the Graves Golf Academy website. It is totally dedicated to Moe Norman. You can't talk to him, but you can see him.

It took several years for that chore-ography to develop naturally and become second nature to Moe. It looks like he walks up to the shot, glances at it, and hits the ball at the target without assessing what he is doing, and the ball goes where it is supposed to go the way he wants it to get there.

People who watched him were mesmerized. I played and practiced with Moe over many decades. I watched very carefully what he was doing. It took a few seconds, maybe four or five, for him to see the shot and hit it.

It boils down to knowing that it is a mind game. You feel what your mind envisions. You see the shot you want to create in its entirety. You believe in it. It is constructed the same way every time for every shot. You know the shot and feel the energy for it in your body and naturally believe in it. So, how do you construct the shot-to-be? That is the question. The more mentally acquired energy you can harvest, the easier all this gets.

You have to know and establish where, exactly, that you want the ball to come to rest. That is the *destination point* but, is it the actual target? No, it isn't, although it would seem to be, and it is the result of being accurate that the ball gets there.

The real target is the apex of the flight of the ball, that place in the sky where it begins its descent and enters free fall. You influence free fall by locating the apex and letting your body feel and see that place in the sky through which you know the ball must travel to find its way to the destination point on the ground. Establish an awareness of the apex-fall line; be balanced for it, see it in your mind, in your vision of the shot-to-be. It comes to mind instantly when you look at the situation of the shot-to-be.

Believe in this as the right shot. Let the body move with ease, never pressuring the hit. Release the mental energy you created and feel easily into your image of the shot-to-be as the face of the club touches and holds the ball momentarily.

Awareness of where the ball leaves the face of the club is the cue that initiates the swing that feels like it happens by itself. It's an effortless exercise physically when it happens that way.

Creating and assembling the image, and feeling for the shot-to-be is a knowing mental use of the power in the creation of thought. *It is true golf.* Once that power, that energy, is felt and used, and its effectiveness revealed, the quest for more is never ending. It goes very deep into the mind's desire. Seek it, and you will find that is true. This is how the swing-to-be actually balances the player for the shot-to-be and establishes what Moe called "the feeling of greatness."

What indeed is the source of all that energy? The more energy you tap into, the more energy you realize there is. There is no apparent limit. It becomes *magic*, and you start using it and seeing it that way.

So, how did Moe and I pursue this? Well, we hit a lot of golf balls and we talked, and we read, and we hit more golf balls. It is a way of life.

In those days in the late 1970s and early 1980s, one of the places Moe and I practiced was the back end of a sports area in New Smyrna Beach, Florida;

another was that private field in Oak Hill south of New Smyrna. It was private also for six very large, suspicious, brahman bulls. We got to know them, sort of. The first day we went there, the cattle eyed us, and we eyed them. We got our clubs from the car trunks and got through the fence into the field. The cattle didn't move. They knew people, but not us.

Moe moved about a millimeter too close, and one of the bulls snorted and pawed the ground, and Moe retreated immediately. The bull relaxed. We stayed where we were and the cattle gradually ignored us and wandered away down the field about two hundred yards to lay down. The grass was short and perfect for hitting balls with trees here and there as targets. We could see the cattle. They were trying to have a mid-morning nap.

Beasts of the Field

Moe poured out his 250 or 300 balls and hit some wedges. The cattle were okay with that. Moe moved to a six iron "to get the swing moving" as he liked to do in his practice regimen. So did I.

The ground in Florida generally, and in this field, is sandy. When the balls landed, there was a thud and six large heads popped up and looked around. It was quiet, no wind, no traffic noise or aircraft like we had at the New Smyrna airport. They relaxed. We each hit another ball. Up came the six heads. They were looking around trying to figure it out. This went on for many, many shots. Moe and I hit our balls away from the bulls to an area near a fence. Then we had to pick up the balls. We proceeded down the field. Moe was edging closer and closer to the fence trying to keep an escape route open. When we got to where the golf balls were and stopped, the cattle stood up.

We had a lot of balls to pick up, and we'd hit them with everything up to a four wood. The balls were all at what we thought was a safe distance from the brahmans. We used our wedges to scoop the balls into the practice bag. They watched, motionlessly, unless either of us got too close. Too close created menacing snorts, pawing the ground, warnings that we had better heed. It was a little dicey, but as the days went by and we came and went, the brahmans ignored us eventually, satisfied that we were no threat.

Our practice area in New Smyrna Beach bordered the airport but did not interfere with it. We were out of the way and hitting balls away from the runways. We hit our own balls and picked them up ourselves. That way we used the same balls we played with, not range balls, and when we picked them up, we could see the grouping with each club we'd used. That way, the margin for error was ascertained and portable to actual playing. It is a practical way to know your capabilities.

There is nothing that keeps people interested that is more effective than a good mystery. The mysterious quest for the way to cause the little white golf ball to arrive at the desired destination point has captured the attention of many millions of people now playing the great game. All of the discussion of the mechanics of the stroke, the swing, down through the decades of golf history have brought us to the present level of expertise, namely, that only a minuscule percentage of those playing golf break the barrier of 100 strokes per round.

In my view, there is no beginner who aspires to play good golf and no one among the upper echelon of professional tour players who would not benefit from the simplicity of Moe Norman's technique of ball striking provided, and this is critical to the success of the effort, that the player's grip is correct. The grip of the club must be in the palm and above the knuckle of the forefinger, and between the heel and the three fingers of the left hand for a right-handed player. The right hand supports the left hand position. The feel in the grip is established so that it accomplishes a *free release* through centrifugal force of the sweet spot of the club face along the intended line. Do not pressure the hit with the hands.

It is unlikely that any of the purveyors of mechanical solutions who do not also begin to convey and disseminate the process of the mental construct which gives rise to the physical motion will alter that sorry statistic of hapless mediocrity. Playing good golf requires determination to master. It can, and does, become a quest that continues.

In the 1950s, the statistic of those breaking 100 was similar to today's figure. Ben Hogan was a king. He and Sam Snead ruled the roost along with Byron Nelson. PGA tournaments were coming prominently into being.

I lived across the road from Pickering Golf Club in Ontario. I looked up to golf pros. I played junior golf tournaments in the summer and hockey in the winter. My brother, Neil, raised chickens and listened to popular music. It was early in life. My father, Scott Young, was a famous Canadian writer and media personality. Neil was not yet famous.

The art of the great game of golf needs to be elevated so that those who take it up do not abandon it; rather, they embrace the game and find the happiness it can offer. Improvement nurtures fascination and breeds enthusiasm.

It is time to take up the discussion of the mental action that drives the entirety of the art of striking the ball and playing the game. It is not enough to say, "visualize the shot" or "picture the shot," then move on to the millionth description of the address position, the takeaway, the reversal, the weight transfer, and so on; but it continues to happen. Consistency in the desired physical motion is derivative of the mental construct. However, the "shot tracker" technology brings a visual component to the televised broadcasts that is useful, that is, if it is utilized thoughtfully. Now, the apex of the flight of the ball is noted. That is good. It's a beginning.

Those in the golf business wish to keep the game alive and growing by nurturing the natural interest of those who take up the game to continue. It is incumbent on the deans of golf to raise the torch that leads the way and define what it is that is the fuel of its flame. Contemplate Ben Hogan's reason for branding his line of irons as Producer, Director, and Apex. The ball striker is the producer and director of the shot-to-be. Recognition of the apex is the cue that creates the thought-form of the whole shot. It radiates that energy throughout the mind and body and is the feeling which manifests as the flight of the ball. I call it "the signal of attachment." The whole body feels the whole shot.

CHAPTER 6
THE APEX

It is my good fortune to understand Moe's knowledge of mechanics and receive that knowledge from him. Moe is widely acknowledged by professional golfers as one of the two finest strikers of the golf ball ever seen—the other being Ben Hogan. Moe was an avid Ben Hogan fan, as am I. However, what is set out here is neither a comparative analysis of Moe Norman's system to the methodology set down by Ben Hogan, nor is it a dissertation on observed similarities and differences in the various positions adopted by each throughout the swing; rather, it is a factual account of my understanding of what causes Moe Norman's method of delivering a direct hit to work and how the mental technique itself emerged into language that now allows a detailed discussion. A "direct hit" is best understood as "direct contact" of the sweet spot of the club face with the centerline of the ball and "the chosen line of aim." It's what Moe meant when he said "centerize yourself." The club face picks up the ball as it goes through to the end of the orbit. It is best understood and learned as a slinging action, not a "hit."

He and I talked and practiced together over the years from the early 1960s to his passing in 2004, sometimes on a daily basis, for several consecutive years in Canada and in the United States in Florida.

Moe acquired the knowledge of how to deliver direct contact over many years of practice and play. A score of 54 is considered a "perfect round" of golf, which has never been done in professional competition. Shooting a 59 or under even once is a major achievement. Moe shot 59 three times. In one of those rounds, he three-putted once, and he did not always putt particularly well, but he hit the ball close to the hole often. Among professional golfers worldwide, he is an icon as a ball striker. His competitive playing record is superb. He is a member of Canada's Golf Hall of Fame.

There is a move in the golf swing that is so pure that the initial vibration of the club face touching the ball can be felt. When that happens, the ball goes to the chosen target, exactly. The motion that produces this requires a creative state of mind that sees and, in effect, dreams the *shot-to-be, the right shot*. A quiet mind is the foundation for this.

I assume this to be the causal body/mind at work with creative power. Moe Norman has had this ability from time to time over many years as an aspect of his talent. Early in his life, he practiced and practiced, and brought it to the foreground of his art. At his best, he shot many upon many scores in competition in the low sixties.

One day in the early 1960s in Florida at Tomoka Oaks Golf Club in Ormond Beach, he hit the flagstick six times in the first nine holes. We were playing together; I watched him do this. It was a magnificent display of precision. It looked easy because it was easy, at least for that particular nine holes. Once, in the early 1980s at Spruce Creek Golf Course in the Daytona Beach area, I hit the flagstick four times in nine holes. It is a good feeling. Moe was impressed. "Make the chosen line of aim. Centerize yourself."

Golfers, being essentially a group held by a common fascination, will likely enjoy acquiring some of the nuggets of information that actually cause the ball to travel from wherever it may be to its chosen destination point. The technique, once clearly understood, is reliable. It is simple. Every shot is assessed and struck employing the same procedure.

It requires some careful consideration to grasp the totality of the technique of assembling the image of the *shot-to-be*. It is totally a mental exercise and an organized form of visualization.

Not many know this, but one so called "swing thought" definitely worthy of serious consideration is particularly effective in developing the correct physical motion. To wit: *Imagine the ball is stuck on the face of the club, and you will wind up and sling it into the flight line. It is very important because it opens the mental door to a natural creation of the image of the flight of the ball, the shot-to-be. The refined mechanics of the physical motion thus created is what Moe Norman did.*

There is, however, another swing thought that Moe and I found useful after I could utilize the one just mentioned. It is also simple: When I envisioned the shot-to-be, I became aware of the end of the finish, that is, the end of the orbit, and I felt the entire motion of what was about to manifest. I held that energy in abeyance and released it into the image when the sweet spot of the club face made direct contact and held the ball momentarily. From that point, the takeaway was triggered by my recognition of the place where the ball would leave the club face. My weight went directly to my right heel. The feel in my right leg was positioned with the end of the orbit, which I recognized and maintained in the takeaway. Moe's weight went directly to his right heel. I asked him about that. I was also aware of the end of the orbit of the motion of the *sweet spot of the* club head. Another critical factor is the grip. A right-handed player's left-hand grip must be such that the shaft is between the thumb and the palm knuckle of the forefinger. Otherwise, a free release is inhibited and centrifugal force is impaired.

In the ready position, I was balanced for and aware of the apex-fall line. For me, it worked. I was "centerized" through the lines of balance upward through each heel and aware of the sweet spot center of the club face, the center of the ball, and the center of the flight line. The feel in my left leg recognized the apex-fall line with the inside leg muscles pulling toward my right, and the inside muscles of my right leg felt the end of the orbit of the sweet spot and did not move to my right in the takeaway. Recognition of the place where the ball leaves the club face triggered the takeaway. At impact in the photograph below, like Moe, my feet are flat on the ground. The T-shirt is a Neil Young and Crazy Horse tour shirt.

Some who read what follows here may view the information given as a breakthrough in the area of the relationship of the mind and the body as it pertains to the game of golf or any endeavor in which there is a target and a projectile launched by a human being. Tennis and archery are two examples. There are many others.

Photo Courtesy of Jan Conner

Every good player, PGA Tour winner, or club champion knows that visualization is important, yet there is no detailed description of a technique for visualization in print. Usually there is the simple admonition to visualize the desired shot. It is good advice, but how, exactly, does one accomplish this?

Neither Moe nor I encountered anyone who teaches a technique that resembles what is suggested in these pages. Moe, who knew most in the game who had something interesting to say, told me nothing like it exists. For years, we speculated on the exact mental technique employed by Ben Hogan, notwithstanding the fact that it involves seeing into the thought processes of another person.

One thing is apparent from the film records: Ben Hogan's flow of motion is the result of a union between his thought processes and his system of physical mechanics. This is also true of Moe Norman and others who from time to time enter the "zone," as it's called, where all goes well.

Here, there is the advantage of knowing Moe's system of mechanics and, as well, the mental procedure he utilizes as best he can describe it. Moe's description is sparse and very precise, as is that of Ben Hogan, as described in his writings. A lot is said in a few words here and there. Understanding the meaning of what is said has been an elusive pursuit within the game, thus, most of the discussion has reverted to physical mechanics.

Anyone wanting to look into Moe Norman's mechanical methodology should examine the Graves Golf Academy site on the internet. Todd Graves is a fervent disciple of Moe Norman. He spent a lot of time with Moe and learned the physical mechanics of his technique. One day back there in the 1990s, Moe told me that if I saw Todd from a couple of fairways away, I would think it was him.

THE APEX CONTINUED

In the summer when the PGA Tour passed through Canada for the Canadian Open, often in the province of Ontario, and in the winter on the swing through Florida on the way to the Masters at Augusta, Moe sometimes appeared at the ropes of the practice tee on the day of the practice rounds. When asked to hit balls, he always obliged. He was the "living legend" in their eyes. He loved to hit balls, thousands of them. He would do it for nothing, and he has. It was bad business, but then business had little in it that was relevant to what made Moe tick.

As he hit ball after ball in his street shoes with unfamiliar equipment belonging to one of those inviting him to give a demonstration, the greats of the game watched in awe. A silence settled over them as their own dreams manifested in the form and flow of the artistic performance they witnessed. No wonder. I watched it all the time. Each stroke flies true. That elusive feeling of ease is so close to all of them now. They can see it and talk to its owner, its friend. Moe, they wonder, how do you do that?

"It's so simple," he says, "watch." And another shot flies to the target.

When he finishes and the show is over and he wanders away, the magic goes with him except for the memories indelibly printed in the minds of the world's greatest players who stood quietly, soaking it up, and looking for the keys to the locks.

Even the term itself, *direct hit*, implies certainty and confidence. Competence is the precursor of confidence. Moe Norman, at the least, was supremely competent, and at the highest, a genius.

"*Centerize yourself,*" said Moe, in response to a question I asked about alignment. Eventually, I did *centerize* myself. In a practical sense, Moe understood how it is that the center of the sweet spot of the club face contacts the center line of the ball and holds it momentarily, then releases it into the center of the flight line *as the mental-energy image of the shot-to-be is released consciously and becomes the shot-that-is*. Once understood, it solves the quest for perfect balance.

That is partly how the perfect shot manifests. It is a *slinging action*. All of this is created and made manifest very quickly *when the mind sees the right shot, creates its image, adopts the ready position, and triggers the feel for the motion of the swing*.

"*Pay attention to what your feet feel*," said Moe, "*not where they are*." Very slightly open is the correct stance.

It happened as a result of *recognizing and feeling the apex of the desired flight of the ball. That is how I got* "centerized." *That is how it jelled*. Sure, I understood the description of the mechanics, but what about the mental technique that caused it to work properly and allowed consistent flow into the swing? That is the real question in golf, the question of causality, both in ball-striking and actual play.

The idea of creating desire, without desire expressed, of the shot-to-be, of holding that desire and releasing it automatically into the shot that is, is the artistry of the mental equation of ball striking. It is the "energy" of it. See the shaft of light in front of the ball into the intended flight path in the photo of me striking the ball.

Moe doesn't approach the ball until he is ready to draw the club back. This part of the choreography indicates that the body is ready and alive to the situation at hand. He is in motion, having first established the image of the right shot, the *shot-to-be*. It is the technique for assembling the image of the right shot, the *shot-to-be*, that imparts to the body the feeling for the whole shot. It happens instantly, not even a few seconds. Thus, is developed the feeling-readiness to draw back the club with certainty. It is easy in that the entire situation of striking the ball has a definite sense of direction that is wholly controlled by the mind's created image of the right shot.

It is the mental state alone that allows the flow and feeling of physical ease that all golfers desire. Competitive players search for this feeling. It is to them, "the zone." They find it elusive. It appears from somewhere from time to time and all goes well; then, it slips quietly away like some forgotten thought or the beautiful stewardess from the last trip to wherever.

For the seeker, it is always just about at hand, over the next mental knoll, around the next corner, maybe. It is always so close, almost within reach; then one day, when your mind is quiet, it touches you, and in touching you, it quietens the mind even further by the depth of certainty it imparts. The ball goes where you wish. Now, how do you find your way back to that state of mind? It took me a lot longer to figure that out than it does to do it.

Today, I am in Florida in New Smyrna Beach, writing this book and incorporating writings and notes from the past forty years. I go to the driving range at the municipal course to hit balls and use the putting green. Gary Wintz is the pro, a good guy who let Moe and I play Spruce Creek for free back in the early 1980s. Yesterday, I strained some of the muscles and/or tendons around my left knee simply because it has been a while since I practiced the kind of move that creates a part of the motion of the swing where the upper body is turning away from the ball and the lower body begins a move in the opposite direction.

I mention this by way of saying that the mental construct created this situation, that is, the mental construct I developed decades ago and Moe and I both used. I noticed this strain in my left knee area when I awoke this morning, but yesterday, when I was hitting tee shots, I could feel the flow of motion and the sense of certainty returning. I knew it was wholly the result of the mental technique.

In 2022, I turned eighty years of age. I know I can play good golf again, and I know why and how to go about it. All you aging baby boomers out there whom I preceded by being born in 1942 should take heart. As Yogi Berra, baseball's great home run hitter, said, "It ain't over 'til it's over and even then, it ain't over."

On the PGA Tour, it is this feeling and flow of certainty that wins. Look at the flow when Steve Ballesteros won the British Open in 1988 at Lytham. Jack Nicklaus captures this, or rather, it has captured him from time to time, to wit, the victory in the 1986 Masters. Then you have the magnificence of Tiger Woods once again starting to emerge in 2018. It was beautiful to watch. And there is that great crew of new stars on the PGA Tour: Rory McIlroy, Justin Thomas, Dustin Johnson, Jordan Spieth, Rickie Fowler, Jason Day, Tommy Fleetwood, Paul Cantlay, and more coming.

When it's right, it feels like the creation of music. The mind and body are one. Together, they move with ease under the same sails, set on the same course; one blows the wind, the other holds the line. The journey is thus traversed, and the ball flies true. Rory McIlroy won at Bay Hill a few days ago. He recaptured the magic. When he looks over his shoulder now, there's Tiger on the road home to the winner's circle. Golf lives.

CHAPTER 7
DANCING THE GREEN

Two things were most valuable to Moe Norman: firstly, his knowledge, and secondly, his personal privacy to pursue more knowledge. He was a lonely individual whose severe childhood contributed to the shy and introverted life he led for many, many years.

To the observer, my friend Moe exhibited some of the characteristics of mild autism. For those familiar with the character played by Dustin Hoffman in *Rain Man*, Moe Norman is not that person. He is a master craftsman, an icon striker of golf balls, and a living legend among competitive players on all professional tours worldwide. The brilliant ball striker, Lee Trevino, on the CBC show *The Fifth Estate*, said in 1988 that "Moe could have won the U.S. Open, all the majors, and he still could." Moe was in his late fifties at the time.

Barry Morrow, the Oscar-winning screenwriter for his work on the major international hit feature film *Rain Man*, has also written a script titled "Dance the Green" about Moe, as well as a foreword for this book. In 2017, Barry conducted several interviews with Canadians who knew Moe and some, like me, that played golf with Moe and practiced with him. Todd Graves of Graves Golf is one of those. It is his company that is assembling a documentary on Moe.

In the summer of 1988 in Ontario, after his winter sojourn in Florida where he was very well known and still remembered, Moe started to hit the ball twenty to forty yards further off the tee depending on weather and ground conditions. His iron shots also increased half a club to a club in distance.

One day, he hit a 360-yard tee shot. I was amazed, but I'd told him in 1980 that long distance and control were within reach for him. This could also be true of anyone who learns the mental technique that Moe and I have discussed over the years. The intricacies of that technique and the theory that supports it is part of the subject of these writings.

Moe has been very good for a very long period of time. At age seventy-three, he held thirty-three course records and had probably won every tournament worth winning in Canada except the Canadian Open. In southern Ontario, where he was known to many but only well known by a few, he spent most of his time with golf professionals and others close to the game.

In his own mind, very few understood him. Sometimes when people who didn't know Moe spoke to him, he walked by them as though they were blades of grass on the fairway. He was a complex blend of genius and childlike simplicity. He loved children, and he loved to hit balls, especially for those fine players on the PGA Tour.

This was an arena where he really shone. He let himself go. In his mind, there was no risk, no danger of the social aftermath of winning on the PGA Tour and becoming visible to the television audience as the finest striker of the ball in the game and the only person seriously compared to Ben Hogan, a man Moe truly admired. He was at ease in what to him was a performance. He was always good.

The tour players gathered around, and the legend grew. When the best of the game saw Moe for the first time, they were not disappointed. Lee Trevino: "If somebody had just taken Moe aside and said, Moe, don't be afraid." I tried that, but it didn't work.

It is very interesting to me to watch the evolution of the physical motion of

Tiger Woods's swing, given my long experience with Moe and my understanding of how to deliver a direct hit. However, it is the mental side of the game, the creative aspect, which drives the action. During the televised press conference from the first day of the 2002 British Open at Muirfield, Scotland, Tiger mentioned the fact that Muirfield offered a variety of ways to get the ball near the flagstick. He was talking about his own enjoyment in having the opportunity and necessity of creating a lot of different shots. In the same vein, he also said you "create the shot, see it, and hit it."

In this writing, I discuss the same thing through my description of the technique of assembling the image and the energy for the *shot-to-be*. It intrigues me because I know that the more refined the execution of the mental construct is, the more efficient and fluid the physical motion becomes, and the quality of the hit then moves through solid and flush into ever-increasing pureness. The swing feels smaller because it is more efficient.

I would have to practice daily over the course of the golf season in Ontario, or months longer, to accomplish that consistency shot to shot, because good physical condition is a cornerstone of athletic performance.

At Augusta in the Masters Championship in 2001, or thereabouts, Tiger Woods hit a nine iron into the green on the eleventh hole. That swing was perfect. The shot was struck like a 145-yard excellent putt. He said it was the best shot he hit in the Masters that year. It obviously sticks in his mind. It is that degree of excellence that Moe Norman exhibited often with all clubs when we practiced and played together. There are certain things that lead to capturing that perfection of ball striking that he and I discussed at length. In short, it was a discussion about causality. Save this writing, there is no record of which I am aware that depicts what I watched and learned with Moe.

In my view, it is the mental action in ball striking and playing the game that is the crux of the game. The creation of "feel" for the *shot-to-be* is the thing to seek. It takes practice but no talent to hold the club properly. Fortunately, everyone can do it. The next thing to know is a clear concept of how to create the image of the desired shot, *the right shot*. Once understood, this provides an exact, clear, sense of direction for the physical motion and makes it far easier to assemble a sound swing or refine one that is already good. *It is, most importantly, the foundation of excellent balance—balance for the* **shot-to-be** *that becomes the* **shot-that-is.**

GET A GRIP ON IT

The grip functions best in the palm of the left hand with the grip of the club on the palm side of the forefinger knuckle. You can see about half the knuckle depending on the shape of your hand. This allows a free release of the club head that maintains a square position to the intended flight line. The right-hand grip, with the armpit pointed up, supports the left-hand position. The left-hand position feels weak to those accustomed to hitting at the ball with their hands. That includes excellent players. However, the objective in the physical motion is a free release that provides optimum use of centrifugal force. The "hit" sensation is eliminated, and it feels like the club face picks up the ball as it's going by and, in effect, slings it effortlessly into the flight line. *Let that happen. You will like the sensation. "LET" is a very important word in striking golf balls. It promotes a free swing, and the hands enjoy the sensation.*

The correct grip is the foundation of excellent balance, and excellent balance eases the creation of a mechanically sound physical motion that is repeatable for all shots and directly related to creation of the image of the shot-to-be.

Once a delving into the use of the power in the creation of thought begins, it does not stop. It may rest for a while, but only long enough for the seeker to figure out how to continue to increase the flow of energy and refine the art of its use. Bring me more of this good thing, you say to yourself. Bring me more energy.

That being said, each advancement and spark of insight that provides a personal enhancement in the use of the power in the creation of thought validates further exploration and discovery. It does not stop, and that is good. As a quest, it can and does bring a lot more to life than one would at first expect to find in the game of golf.

Access to this energy grows and it is portable to other areas of endeavor. Now, for instance, I use my access to energy to write these words, to provide the words that suit the meaning of what I feel so that I can be understood. Communicating this information and knowledge I have gained is enjoyable. Clarity in the mind of the reader is the "*destination point*" for the feeling of what I know.

I ignite the flow of words when it feels right; thus, in another way I have developed my own technique for triggering the written expression. Upon occasion, but not for public consumption, I can do the same thing with a piano, or guitar, and sing along with myself especially if one or the other of these instruments is available to me on a daily basis.

Underlying this knack of personal expression, I feel a strong predilection to set out this work. It has to do with golf but is obviously larger than that and includes experience within life itself. Moe Norman also knew this and probably still does. Death of the body is not death of the soul. The soul goes on forever.

It might surprise some to find out what a spiritual being Moe could be at his best, and with simple eloquence, he could say something profound and heartfelt. He knew what it was to be different, and he knew he was different. He knew what it was to be ostracized. To his last day, he knew what it was to be alone. He knew poverty. He knew what it was to be excellent, to have a talent that he expressed superbly.

By 2002, he also knew personal wealth. Among the books he read were certain volumes of the "I Am Discourses," published by The St. Germain Foundation. They are about life and what it really offers. The world of people has problems, serious problems, insane wars and all the rest of it.

Moe looked at it and played golf. "People don't love each other," he said. "They don't know who they are."

It is my view that Tiger Woods, in his own way, is stalking the same degree of excellence as a ball striker that Moe continued to exhibit often, and that a meeting of the minds between these two individuals would have been very beneficial to Tiger Woods. I think that what Tiger Woods seeks is drawn to him by the very way he goes about finding what he wants. I believe he is creating a life in which the things are drawn to him that he desires to know. It is fascinating to watch this unfold. To me, it is a natural extension of all this that Tiger is doing something about providing access to the game of golf to inner city youth and others without access. That is constructive action.

Several years ago, I wrote a plan that involved corporate America in general, and the golf industry itself, with a mechanism that includes the entertainment industry. In it, a mentor group of professionals from all professions would be available to inner city youth in large metropolitan jurisdictions. It would also include the participation of city governments and enlist the active participation of street organizations. It is constructive action that I would like to see on an international basis some day

When I hit a particularly good shot, one that Moe liked, he'd say, "Whatever you did there, whatever you did there." Sometimes he'd repeat it several times. He meant what I held in my mind. He always said, "You have to have a quiet mind." The rest came after that. "Centerize yourself" and "make the chosen line of aim" were fundamental aspects to him. The activity of the mind was what held his attention.

In Moe Norman we have a natural human resource, a rare individual who knows how to deliver a direct hit on a golf ball. Only a few are close to that degree of expertise. Moe's talent is visibly in a class alone. Purity of technique was his ongoing quest, his method of improvement. His genius continues to be an inspiration to me.

He is a paradox to observers who see his artist's grace as an accomplished master against the social reticence that until the late 1980s and early 1990s thwarted a financially successful career. The money aside, Moe Norman has risen to a rarified atmosphere when it comes to the game of golf. His expertise is respected. He knew that and appreciated it, and in return for this recognition, he was very unselfish with what he knew.

In 1987 at the Canadian Open, Moe hit about a thousand balls, mostly with a driver and a three iron. The PGA Tour professional onlookers dug in their pockets and gave him a few hundred dollars. They were glad of the opportunity to watch him. The next day, they played for a slice of the 600,000-dollar purse. Moe needed that few hundred dollars, but he would have done it for nothing.

When competitive players watch Moe, they know that if they were to acquire his expertise and ability to execute, that only those who could accomplish the same thing would have a chance of beating them over the long haul or, maybe, day to day. Essentially, that is accurate. However, most often it comes down to putting in competition, and if the same mental technique is to be utilized on the greens as applies in the long game, the physical mechanics of delivering a direct hit with a putter must be understood and become second nature.

CHAPTER 8

THE SHOT-TO-BE

Moe spent a lot of time on the putting green. The roll of the putt does indeed tell all, as does the flight of the ball. It is the manifestation of the mind's image whether born of fear or cool professionalism. The technique in putting is portable to the rest of the game, that is to say, that finding the target exactly is the obvious objective of putting. It is that exactness, that tuning to the target, which is portable to all other shots. Aiming is therefore a major component of delivering a direct hit. How, indeed, does one aim, is the question. It is a concept closely aligned with Shakespeare's line, "to be or not to be," and that is not a frivolous statement.

The technique of assembling the image and energy of *the shot-to-be* that Moe and I discuss utilizes the increased energy that becomes available for use mentally as the technique of delivering a direct hit is assimilated. The motion of the full swing and putting stroke can become a foregone conclusion. The flight of the ball and the roll of the putt then become the exclusive intent of the mind's focus.

The Focus of Attention:

The ball I see in my mind is invisible to the observer; it is already at the chosen destination point on the fairway or the hole itself. I am balanced for that and not the ball in front of me. My attention and balance is fixed on the apex-fall line to the destination point I have chosen. I wind up from that point and keep winding up through the reversal until the release happens by itself. There is no need to use the hands to force the club head to get to the contact point in the right position. Rather, the club head picks up the ball as it is going by and slings it effortlessly into the flight line.

In my image, I see the magnetic draw of the "invisible" ball pulling the visible ball through the flight line, to itself. From an inner perspective, I see the ball's invisible energy and place it at the chosen destination point. The point to all this is that it is consistent with the desire to get the ball to go where you choose it to be.

I save the energy of the creation of the shot-to-be. It is like desire without desire expressed, and it is delivered like an explosion into the image as the club face touches and holds the ball momentarily and the shot-to-be manifests in physical reality. I know this will happen, and it is this "knowingness" that achieves absolute focus of attention, and the body moves in accordance with creating the desired flight of the ball.

Where your attention is fixed, you become fixed as well. It is the same for all shots regardless of which club is used or what the distance may be. The mental/physical construct is always the same and adapts intrinsically to the particular requirements of each assembled image of a shot-to-be.

It is, however, beneficial to comprehend the mental technique and the physical mechanics together for the simple reason that the mental technique imparts to the physicality the sense of certainty of direction that creates ease. Alignment ceases to be a mystery. Mental comprehension is the glue that imparts knowingness and flow to the physical motion; in that way, certainty begets ease, and distance and accuracy are one and the same thing. The chosen target and flightpath to *the destination point* becomes all. The flight of the ball tells all.

On the green, the target is relatively close, yet it is elusive. Then one day, it isn't elusive and most putts drop into the hole. What happens in that happy circumstance can be captured and used in the long game; similarly, insights gained from practicing with a driver can be applied in putting. It is a matter of what is noticed during practice and what, in fact, it is that forms the individual golfer's conceptual base. The conceptual core of the knowledge explained here recognizes that mental influence is the crux of shot making and playing the game, but more, it taps that world of mental energy and increases the flow.

Once the physical mechanics of

delivering a direct hit are understood and integrated, then a flow of energy, which is the creation of the thought itself of the *right shot*, becomes the focus of intent. The apex is located and felt. That feeling is the signal of attachment that instantly reveals and triggers formation of the image of the flight of the ball. Thus, is the *shot-to-be* assembled. A good flow of energy comes about then that is similar to the feeling of sureness and certainty that all good players occasionally experience. How do you find that feeling? What is it? These are questions Moe and I pursued relentlessly. The answers always provide the opportunity to learn more and improve. There are degrees of everything.

Execution of the mechanics of a direct hit was a foregone conclusion every day when Moe practiced. He hit the ball on a variety of chosen trajectories at will, all the time. It was as though he had a dial that he adjusted with his eyes. That was the standard I watched. It was pointless to compare the consistency and pureness of his ball striking ability with anyone other than Ben Hogan.

To my eye, Ben Hogan had flow, oneness, in his swing. Moe was a Ben Hogan fan. He often mentioned Byron Nelson and Sam Snead, both of whom he obviously admired, as well as George Knudson, another great Canadian ball striker, whose game blossomed after Ben Hogan kindly spent the time with him that George needed.

These days, at his best, it is my view that Tiger Woods is exhibiting the same degree of excellence. When he is not at his best, errant tee shots put him in some very interesting (to the TV viewer) locations; however, he is great out of trouble. His mind is focused absolutely on the flight line that gets the ball to where he has decided it is going. Once in trouble, that absolute focus seems easier to acquire because now it is an absolute necessity. The ball is not in the middle of the fairway, it is in long grass, there are trees and water to navigate. The mind's focus is the rescuer.

Errant tee shots enjoy a myriad of complications from losing the ball to hitting it from shallow water to confrontations with reptiles like alligators, water moccasins, and rattle snakes in Florida. Hitting the ball with a driver to the right destination point sets up scoring potential that is easier than shots around trees and from the rough.

It has always seemed to me that accurate tee shots are more consistent if the club face is released down the intended line of flight. The shallow finish appears to me by comparison to be much more likely to produce inaccurate shots. The swing should be executed so that the motion of the body moves through the reversal and continues through the actual point of release with the feeling of "letting it happen." That way, there is ease and flow. The speed of the motion is comfortable. See everything prior to release as "controlled" wind-up.

Look carefully at Tiger's best drives and see the oneness and overall coherence of the motion and you will see what I mean. Other players also exhibit this. It is easy to get distracted by mechanics, even for great players. When Tiger's back is against the wall and he's trying to come from behind to win, he is great.

To me, it appears that his mind becomes glued like a magnet to the way the ball is going to go where he wants it to be. He can make it happen. It is a pleasure to watch him, and it is obvious to me he can be better. Moe Norman's understanding of accuracy would be a helpful addition to what Tiger and others on the PGA Tour already know.

Until there is a coherent mental technique from which flows a refined general perception of perfect mechanics, there will be but a few who come to grasp the keys to excellence. Conversely, the dissemination of a sophisticated and simple mental technique that is understandable and useable by all who aspire to play golf would bring very quickly or, at the least, engender a wave of high-level players that would raise the bar significantly on performance standards.

Most of the misinformation on mechanics would fall by the wayside. The standard used by instructors would be upgraded and predicated on the fact that the mind instigates everything that occurs that produces the flight of the ball.

Ben Hogan advised George Knudson not to put his hands on the grip until he was ready to draw back the club. That way, the "feel" for the shot-to-be was already established and the feel in the hands agreed with it and radiated certainty. When the feel in your hands is certain, it eases the entire motion of the swing.

It is best to understand the motion of the swing as a revolving action constituted of wind-up and release. Its physical platform is the balance itself established in the "ready position" in accordance with the feeling created and held by assembling the energy of the image of the shot-to-be. It is "the signal of attachment" to the apex that reveals the image and radiates the feeling and flight line for the shot-to-be.

The signal of attachment reveals itself when the eyes rise from the exact chosen destination point for the flight of the ball until the apex of the flight, the place where the ball begins its descent, is sensed, felt physically, and realized mentally. It happens instantly.

The eyes then come back along the flight line, inhaling the shot-to-be, so to speak, to a point where the motion of the swing is triggered by seeing and sensing the place where the ball leaves the face of the club. The entirety of the flight line is clear in the mind. Imagine the ball's energy is at the destination point and is drawing the ball in front of you to itself. Imagine the ball in front of you is stuck on the face of the club. Sense the mass of the club head with a recognition of the sweet spot that includes the energy of the image of the shot-to-be and know that it is this energy in the mind that is released as the club face touches and holds the ball momentarily. Think of it as a slinging action, because that is what it is. Never pressure the hit.

When you practice with a driver, for instance, and you want to increase distance, ascertain the location of the last perfect shot you hit, say your longest accurate shot, and extend the image by five feet and be precise with that. Watch what starts to happen, say, over the course of a month. Gradually, your average distance will increase given that the swing's motion produces a direct contact, and no added physical force is required or felt. It is my view that a sophisticated mental construct eases the flight of the ball. I did this in the early 1980s practicing with Moe in Oak Hill, Florida. It was fascinating.

There is a dance-like coherence to the physical choreography of arriving in the ready position that is derivative of the assembling of the image of the shot-to-be. In the creation of thought, which is what this is, there is a great deal of power. Each time a shot-to-be is conceived and launched, there is an opportunity to practice the mental technique and hone it down into the fine art that is its potential. Eventually, that is how I practiced and will again when I start hitting a lot of balls prior to the release of this book.

To accomplish this, an understanding of the actual simplicity of the physical mechanics needs to exist.

A great many fine players have decided, incorrectly in my view, that the principles Moe used are unique to Moe and do not apply to others. It is true that over his career with his outstretched arms and the straight-legged (but not locked) wide stance that others find looks awkward and therefore impossible to duplicate, that the simple principles upon which his system is based have been obscured, and the potential value of its general applicability, diminished.

Moe's methodology of mechanics is not a standard referred to as a benchmark except in these writings and on the Graves Golf Academy website. However, great players have watched the masterful ball striking and the perfect flight of the ball. They could win anything, any tournament, with that know-how, if they knew how to acquire it.

The explosion of interest in golf among the youth of our society attributable to the efforts and success of Tiger Woods early in his career and many others before him, plus the great new young players of today like Jordan Spieth, Rickie Fowler, Justin Thomas, Dustin Johnson, and all their contemporaries, would be well-served by an accurate account of the simplicity and excellence of the principles of Moe Norman's system of mechanics and the mental construct that supports it.

In Moe's stance, which is slightly open, his feet are slightly outside his shoulders. His extended arm position and straight legs at address establish his upper body angle. In the reversal, his knees bent automatically to deliver the club head directly down the line. It is the principles of his system that are applicable on an individual basis and, if nothing else, playing golf is an individual pursuit. What he did that day with me in New Smyrna Beach, Florida on the practice range at the municipal golf club was the culmination, a milestone or life-stone, of a life of dedication to excellence in his chosen endeavor.

Any beginner employing Moe Norman's system of mechanics will circumvent much of the confusion propagated by the miasma of technical data and descriptions now on the market in instructional books and videos, and on daily golf broadcasts. There is nothing intentionally wrong or misleading in the methodologies extant. It is the honest and enthusiastic pursuit of the growing many who pursue the "secret"—the "way" to get the little white ball from wherever it is to the location chosen.

It isn't that all discussion of physical mechanics would cease if Moe Norman's system were widely employed. Rather, it would be reduced to useable fact because of its simplicity and the directness, learned by the student, of the effect of the mental technique on the physical motion. This is equally true of the accomplished player and the novice.

Acquiring the personal use of the technique requires that the mechanics of delivering direct contact must be understood. Reading books like this one— that is, if there are any others—is useful up to a point. At the highest levels, it is obviously best to have personal access to an acclaimed master, or someone who can articulate and demonstrate the technique in order to acquire the refinements of the art. George Knudson sought out and found Ben Hogan. The knowledge he gained brought his long game up to a superb level, and he won on the PGA Tour.

In the late 1970s, it became possible for me to spend several years in succession practicing and playing with Moe Norman. It provided the way, finally, for me to ask the right questions and find the answers. The knowledge imparted in such a forum has a personal flow to it that is naturally tailored to the seeker of the knowledge. Moe showed me what works. He never talked about what didn't work. "Why bother," he'd say. "If you do, then the ball goes there where you don't want it."

In Moe's view, the average golfer has two things in mind: namely, hope and fear. To practice as I did, with a master striker of the ball, allowed certain things about ball striking to become apparent. My experience with Moe was a rare opportunity, captured. It is unusual in any pursuit to have lengthy access to a great talent. That type of individual enjoys and needs solitude. However, like other people, they also have friends and confidants with whom they discuss the finer points of their particular profession. Moe knew absolutely how to deliver the center of the club face along the center of the flight line. The ball goes straight. "What's wrong with straight?" Moe used to say.

Moe Norman explained to me as best he could his system of mechanics. The mental technique, its terminology and description, I developed myself as a way of explaining it to myself. Moe's use of the phrases "centerize yourself" and "make the chosen line of aim" are two gems of "golf oil" that I find gain greater significance as time goes on. Another of Moe's gems is *"imagine the ball is stuck on the face of the club."*

"Not many know this," he told me.

All by itself, this thought promotes the correct physical motion. It promotes swinging from the heels, from the ground upward. It is very, very, important.

Imagine that the invisible center of the sweet spot of the club face is glued to the invisible centerline of the ball, and you are revolving and keeping that ball stuck to the club face as you wind up and through the point of release. You never want to let it go. If you do this, the ball will fly along the chosen flight line, each time, provided that the energy of the image of the shot-to-be is properly assembled and triggers the physical motion, and your grip is correct.

Assemble the energy of the image of the shot-to-be and deliver that energy into the image. The energy of which I speak flows in through the mind and it is confirmed through the invisible vertical lines of balance up from the earth through a certain point in each heel. Feel that and know true balance. Rebuild your swing from there. Let it happen. Let your grip change if it wants to so that the heel of the left hand and the palm are in control with one knuckle visible, and let the right-hand position support the left-hand position without tension or tightness. Let freedom into the motion. The perfect shot is effortless; the almost-perfect shot is easy. You start from wherever you are: someone with a 14 handicap or a beginner, maybe one of those players knocking on the PGA Tour's door wanting to qualify for the Tour and win.

CHAPTER 9
THE MAGIC OF PUTTING

PUTTING: THE FIRST FRONTIER

The long game, the short game, and putting define the unfolding order of play on every hole played by every golfer on every golf course worldwide, forever. The only variable apart from the weather is the mindset of each and every player on the field, the conscious presence of each one of them, now and forever.

Each one looks at the shot or putt and wants the ball to go to the target. If each were to remember and save the feeling itself of the shot or putt that is perfect and become accustomed to doing that so it could be reproduced more often, then both the average and accomplished player's performance would improve. The desire to produce consistent repetition is the reason terminology was developed to describe *assembling the feel for the shot-to-be*.

Putting is an excellent area of the game to develop the knack for remembering and reproducing the feeling for the perfect shot, and there is a great deal to be said for the idea of assembling an efficient golf game by learning early how to putt and to understand the relevance of the art of putting to the rest of the game. The distances are short and always within reach. It isn't 250 yards into the wind and rain on a cool day. It is within normal capabilities to hit a perfect putt, and excellent putting removes pressure from the long game. The know-how of good putting is portable to other areas of the game. Putting is also where a lot of money is won and lost in the friendly game and on the PGA Tour.

There are few freely moving putting strokes visible anywhere. The techniques of the long putter and the shoulder-controlled strokes are effective to a degree. There is little real freedom to them. The hands, despite their fineness of sensitivity, have come to play a severely diminished role. The next PGA Tour player with a free putting stroke, someone with a personal grasp of the mental technique necessary to lock the ball into the target, could dominate.

Learn to assemble the image of the roll-line of the putt-to-be and watch what starts to happen.

On the PGA Tour in the United States, the greens are very fast and essentially true. They are as close to perfect as possible for the purposes of putting. It isn't inconceivable for a master putter to arrive on the competitive scene and consistently produce scores across four rounds of between twenty-five and thirty under par, unless the courses are deliberately "tricked up" so that greens reject good shots and the rough is unfair.

Meanwhile, the greens are very fast, and the putter head must move slowly and accurately; thus, the shoulder stroke and its defensive tone. Why move the shoulders to hit the ball a few feet? As with the long game, it is essential to have the correct grip to allow a free release. It is also necessary to have a clearly defined mental construct that produces a feeling of certainty and knowingness.

Establishing the correct pressure points in the putting grip is the precursor to developing a highly refined action for the motion of the sweet spot of the club head. The mechanical objective is a duplicate of the principles of a full swing, minus the weight transfer and lateral weight shift.

The goal is to deliver the center of the sweet spot of the putter head along the center of the roll line, consistently. The correct grip produces a putting stroke with very few moving parts. It allows superb accuracy and control of power. It is repeatable because its design is sophisticated, and it works. The mind directs the action and creates the feel that the sensitivity of the hands can use and repeat effectively.

PUTTING AND THE ART OF THE DIRECT HIT.

Explanation of The Grip And Pressure Points Used By A Master Putter: Alvie Thompson, a Canadian PGA Champion

The Grip

The heels of both hands press inward with even pressure toward each other, and the middle two fingers of each hand pull with even pressure in the opposite direction to one another. The thumbs press evenly downward.

When the stroke is initiated, the butt end of the putter moves forward and then naturally returns to a position to the right of the original vertical starting position of the stroke. It is a pendulum action that is created. The pressure points in each hand are doing the same thing, namely, manifesting the perfect stroke for the putt at hand.

On short putts, it is a slight amount the butt end moves, on a longer putt, further to the right in the follow through. For a left-handed stroke, it is the opposite.

An excellent way to practice this is to establish an absolutely flat surface on a putting green or a carpet in your home. Place a ten-cent piece as the target. Mentally place the ball on top of the coin.

ASSEMBLING THE IMAGE AND FEEL FOR THE PUTT-TO-BE:

Establish the exact destination point and awareness of:

- **The Sweet Spot of the Putter**
- **The Center of the Ball**
- **The Center of the Roll Line of the Putt**
- **Sense of the Force of the Blow**

*NOTE: CONNECT THE CENTERS

First, sense the mass of the putter and the invisible center of the putter's sweet spot by holding the putter head off the ground and feeling its weight.

Bounce a ball off the putter face to find the exact center of the "sweet spot". Retain this sense.

It is this sense of the mass and the invisible center of the sweet spot that is delivered through the center line of the ball and into the center of the roll line of the *putt-that-is*. The objective is to connect the centers.

The force of the blow varies from one stroke to another; however, the design of the methodology of assembling the image and feel for the putt-to-be incorporates automatically the force of the required blow and determines the length of the stroke necessary to deliver it. I feel that in my fingertips. That is where it registers and triggers the stroke. It is a slightly descending blow.

The whole body feels the whole putt. It gathers the feel from the creative mental process. Learn to trust the assembled feel and let the stroke happen as though by itself. Your mind will sense when the energy assembled is ready, and your hands will move, and the stroke will happen. It is effortlessness in action.

If you doubt that this is so, then contemplate what actually happened the last time you looked at a putt and knew that it would go in the hole, then struck it, and it did go in the hole. Somehow, you let that happen.

What I am suggesting here and in the long game is that it is possible to understand and recreate the procedure that allows this "magic" to be repeated. Give your brain and mind a chance. All the mechanical descriptions of how to putt and play the long game can be lined up end to end, maybe circle the globe, and then continue to bypass totally the lure of recreating the "magic" of that great feeling of knowingness and certainty.

Golf is not played by mechanics alone. It isn't that or nothing. Give *Mind Power* a chance. It can bring peace and quiet, and freedom and ease to your golf game or, as Moe put it, "the feeling of greatness."

Moeism (2003)

"I just learned to putt a short time ago, and now I putt so well it would make you cry. It's the best part of my game, and that's saying a lot."

Moe Norman, at age seventy-three, has found that freedom and peace and ease. He loves it and you could learn to love it too. It has permeated his entire golf game. The little bit of information I gave him improved his balance, he says, and that made everything easier in putting and the long game. Now, in 2003, Moe Norman's stance is on the wide side of conventional, and his finish is full. He is the finest striker of a golf ball to be found anywhere today, for my money, and he just got better. I am pleased to have seen that happen.

A few others also saw this happen, but Moe only lived another year or so.

TRY THIS:

*Visualize the ball's energy being intercepted by the hole.

*The eyes look from beyond the hole where the visualized and imagined ball's energy is placed mentally, then back to the location of the ball and never from the ball to the hole.

*In assessing the line and the roll of the whole putt, observe the line from the low side (on a breaking putt) from a point midway between the hole and the ball.

*Balance yourself for *the destination point of the ball's energy*, either in the hole on a short putt or slightly beyond the hole on a longer putt where there is the necessity of diminishing the effect of irregularities on the putting surface around the hole.

*Result: the sense of the required force of the blow is felt and naturally determines the length of the stroke.

I notice the feeling registers in my fingertips and instantly, and naturally, initiates the stroke, and the stroke happens with ease.

One of the reasons, and there are others, that so many putts come up just short of the hole and perfectly on line is that the player's visual focus is centered on the near side of the hole rather than from a point slightly beyond the hole and, from there, back to the location of the ball. The result is that the player picks up a sense of the force of the blow based on where his or her attention is centered. Where your attention is, there are you. Simple, isn't it, unless you've never thought of it that way.

Televised broadcasts of the PGA Tour events are perceived to be the first and last word on the great game and never mention this as a major item in all the statistical data. Why is this so? The answer may be that there is no comprehension of this point that any player who understands it is willing to discuss openly. It is not a secret, but it does provide a competitive edge, a very serious competitive edge.

On the PGA Tour and other professional tours, how much money has been lost by putts right on line but woefully, woefully, short? Over the years, millions and millions of dollars. Next week, a few more millions of dollars. It adds up. On the LIV Tour, it will add up even faster.

CHAPTER 10
PLAYING THE GAME AGAIN

Now, from my home in New Smyrna Beach, Florida, I will go to the golf course and the practice range, often. I am there to take a free swing and get the "magic" back. I want to get into good physical condition, play the game, and hit the golden shot. The best part is I know I can do it, despite the fact that I am eighty-plus years of age. To accomplish this, I can only use what I know. In a nutshell, this is what I know. You can take it to the Golf Bank. So, all you baby boomers out there who are wondering what to do, don't worry. You've got me by at least ten to fifteen years. Bear in mind again, the words of Yogi Berra: "it ain't over 'til it's over and even then, it ain't over."

Yesterday, I hit fifty-five balls, twenty with wedges, ten with seven irons, and twenty-five with five irons. The wedges were about eighty yards aimed at a pole approximately the size of a telephone pole. I hit the pole the first three shots and, of the next seventeen shots, four more times. The rest were very close. The seven irons were generally on the line except for two of them, and four or five of them were within six feet of the piece of paper that was the target. Another pole was the five-iron target. It was too far away to hit in the air into the wind. Five of the shots were perfectly on the line. Another ten or twelve were within ten to fifteen feet of the line, and the rest, twenty to twenty-five feet. All went about the same distance. The shots that were on the line all occurred for the same reason: namely, a coherent assembling of the energy of the image of the shot-to-be.

I sensed the sweet spot of the wedge, the seven iron, and the five iron just as I do with the putter, and that, along with my feeling of balance up through my heels, was included in the ready position. All of this is within my awareness while the focus of my attention is on the apex-fall line of the flight of the ball to the chosen destination point. I turned away from the apex, and the feel for that was triggered by sensing the place where the ball leaves the club face. My takeaway is then initiated by a slight forward press with my right knee that sets and recognizes the place where the ball leaves the club face, and my weight goes to my right heel. That is how I am able to deliver the center of the sweet spot through the center of the ball and the center of the flight line as far as my arms can extend.

I know how to establish the exact destination point for the ball's flight the same way for all shots, every time without exception, so that I see the flight of the ball, or the roll-line of the putt, before it happens.

The system I use allows me to establish and be aware of a consistent reality and presence of my own swing the same way every time so that my whole body feels the whole shot. The intent of my swing is absolutely consistent because it conforms to the assembled image and individuality of each shot-to-be.

Since it is the same procedure each time, it allows the true mechanics of the physical motion to be revealed and learned, felt and used, and, with consistent application, to become second nature. Forget so-called muscle memory. Unlike mental memory, it is non-existent. The mind remembers and enjoys a comfortable and familiar physical sensation, and the muscles feel that comfort.

I learned the physical mechanics of delivering a direct hit from Moe and gradually assimilated the information he gave me. I hit hundreds of thousands of full shots with him, and a multitude of putts and greenside short-game shots, and we played golf several times a week off and on for several decades.

Among competitive players on all pro tours, Moe is an icon. It was a privilege for me to spend that time with him. So, now I use what I know. It is very simple and very effective. I don't have to hit another few hundred thousand balls, nor would anyone wishing to learn and use the technique set out here. As I recreate my own golf game and chronicle my progress, it will become evident that anyone who wishes to learn can do it too. I can make this very easy to follow.

The video production that may accompany this book will help anyone truly interested in playing better golf, anyone who wants to qualify for the PGA Tour, the LPGA Tour, or any other professional tour. To do that, he or she needs some very powerful medicine, and I've got some. It is called GOLF OIL. It is the good kind. It works. Remember, I spent all that time with Moe, and there are those little gems of information that ooze out of these geniuses from time to time. I've got a few of them to pass on to you. I call those little gems, "golf oil." They help create certainty and swing-flow.

THE GOLF OIL CORPORATION is in the energy business—mental energy, that is. I selected the company name to avoid confusion.

JUNE 6, 2002

I met my friend, Moe, this morning at Carlisle Golf Club a few miles north of Burlington, Ontario, in Canada. He looked good. We talked for about forty-five minutes in the clubhouse restaurant. It was a pleasant, brief, reunion. We agreed to meet again.

In Moe's world, some friends are now gone, deceased, or getting older and unable to move about as freely. Other things have changed as well. Now, he has money, lots of it, more than he has ever had and more is coming. "I've got almost a million saved, Bob." A few years ago, and for several years prior to that, he had little money and lived what would seem a lonely life to most. That lonely part hasn't changed. I know him, and I can see it in his expression and hear it in his voice. He still lives in a motel near Kitchener, Ontario during the golf season in Canada and a rented room in the Daytona Beach, Florida area in the winter months. He eats in buffet style restaurants and the occasional upscale favorite spot from time to time. In Ontario, he now does about thirty clinics a season and plays nine holes with his longtime friend, Nick Weslock, a multi-time Canadian Amateur champion, several times a week.

All Moe ever wanted to do was play golf, and he did, and he did it very well, and he still does. Moe always points to Sam Snead and Byron Nelson as well as Ben Hogan and Lee Trevino as great ball strikers, but he also knows how good he is. Moe has long since figured out how to create maximum accurate acceleration with the least motion. He knows exactly what he is doing. He says little and makes his words count.

The success of The Golf Channel came up. I asked him if he watched it and pointed out that it has been good for the game in bringing to the public coverage of tournaments that would not otherwise have had exposure, the Canadian Tour being a perfect example. Moe and I had played the Canadian Tour in its infancy. Moe thinks The Golf Channel's instructional material is repetitive, nothing but mechanics. I agree for the most part, but I'd rather watch that than war news and other forms of pain on CNN.

Moe wants to talk about the mental side of the game, "but," he said, "they [The Golf Channel's producers] don't want that. They want what they're doing... your hands here, your feet there, your shoulders this way, this and that...." His voice trailed off and he waved his hand in disdain. It's the same Moe I've always known, just like a child, dead honest.

I needed a new set of irons, so I asked him what's good. "Mizuno," he said, "nothing else is close." I thought to myself, but said nothing, that he's signed with Mizuno competitor Natural Golf. A few tables away, a mother and small child sat down. Moe's attention was immediately drawn to the child, and he rolled a ball across the rug toward them trying to get a rise out of the child. The child was not into it.

I suggested that the mental side of ball striking needs a description with the specific terminology that allows an ongoing discussion to get started. I pointed out that the way it is now, the words "visualize" and "picture" are about as far as it has gotten. It is known to both of us that I was working on a written description of the mental action twenty years ago.

I told him about this book I'm writing and that I'll let him read it when it is finished. He always liked to read what I wrote years ago about golf, and he seemed interested in the idea. He still has copies of the handwritten pages that I gave him.

Moe looked good. "Lost thirty (pounds)," he said. "Don't eat unless you're hungry. Took four months, Bob, four months, yup. Ate the same things, just not as much." Moe Norman is now seventy-three years of age. His birthday is July 10.

I told him there was a good chance that a video production would happen in conjunction with the book I want to publish. Then he mentioned an attractive offer for the film rights to his life. I would like to see that happen. It is exactly what I had in mind in the early 1990s. A major documentary production is the right move with Moe Norman. It would create an historical marker in the game of golf. The life and times of a notable figure in the emerging sport of the masses deserves an accurate record. It would be a major undertaking and a worthwhile one.

I could see this coming in 1992 or 1993, and I had enlisted the assistance of

my brother, Neil, whose career as a sing-
er-songwriter-rock and roller has established him as an icon in his own profession as a solo concert performer and with
the band Crazy Horse and his history with
Crosby, Stills, Nash and Young. Neil's
manager, Elliot Roberts, told me then
that he thought Warner Brothers would
get involved. Although the production
never materialized, telling Moe's story is
perhaps an even more worthy cause now,
given the explosion of interest in the
wonderful game of golf and the significant benchmark Moe has established.

Moe Norman, the person, is one
thing; his degree of expertise in this great
game is another matter. Early in life, he
was ostracized by the elite of the Royal
Canadian Golf Association. In my view,
the RCGA's attitude was reprehensible
and cruel when it could have been benev-
olent and considerate of a talented, albeit
unusual, personality who had something
of value to bring to the game. Many years
ago, I suggested to Lorne Rubenstein, the

noted Canadian golf writer, and others within the professional and amateur ranks in Canada that perhaps Moe was mildly autistic. Nobody disagreed even though it may not be clinically accurate.

The people who ran the RCGA did not accept Moe. He did not have the social grace they expected. They thought he might embarrass them, and that concern was far more important in their eyes than anything else. To them, Moe was a question mark. They put him down and solved their problem by revoking his amateur status.

It hurt Moe deeply, but he kept going, and others within the game who were members of the CPGA, people who liked Moe, accepted him and were able to live with the fact that Moe was an unusual human being who possessed the talent of a genius. Among that group, which is too numerous to list completely, were Moe's great friend, Nick Weslock, George Clifton, Murray Tucker, Lloyd Tucker, Gary Cowan (a two time U.S. Amateur champion), Gus and Audrey Maue and the entire Maue family, Alvie Thompson (a CPGA champion), Bill Wakeham, George Knudson, the Membry family of Gilford, Ontario, Michael Whitney, and virtually every other competitive golfer who ever encountered him.

I spent as much time with Moe as anyone, probably a lot more than most over the years. It was interesting to watch him gradually come out of his shell and try to do the things with other people that represented "socializing" in his mind. I encouraged him by including him, by having dinner with him and treating him as a social equal, and I continued to enjoy his company for the rest of his life.

Moe's legacy among professional touring players is his obvious mastery as a ball striker. That fact will gain prominence when those players realize how he accomplished what they desire to grasp mentally and exhibit publicly in competition. A beginning golfer who knows nothing of the physical mechanics has possibly an easier time assimilating the mental process that is Mind Golf than does the experienced player, simply because there are no preconceived habits to remove or amend. Said Moe, "you have to have a quiet mind." Figure out how to create that quietness and add the physical motion to it.

Moe's legacy with those who knew him will vary from person to person. Craig Shankland, the USPGA Teacher Of The Year in 2001, hosted about 19 years of clinics with Moe mostly in Florida. Several hundred people attended each of those events. They were in awe of what Moe could exhibit. In one such gathering, Craig recalled fondly how he looked at Moe and said, "what's it like to hit perfect shots all the time, Moe?" Moe paused and looked at the spectators and smiled. "You," he said to Craig, "will never know."

My personal recollections of my time with Moe are many. They come to mind often and are mentioned here and there in this book, but now, I notice his presence when I'm at the golf course on the putting green; for instance, as I was practicing one day, Moe popped into my mind with a suggestion for my "ready position." It worked. The pendulum action I use in putting was eased. It brought to mind another of Moe's Moeisms about ball striking: "Don't put no *fierce* on it." So, from my perspective, the "Old Moeski," as I called him, lives on. As Kahlil Gibran, the Lebanese prophet said "let the Earth take her own the soul goes on forever." Telepathic communication bridges the gap.

ABOUT THE AUTHOR

Bob Young was born in Toronto, Ontario, Canada in 1942. He was a member of the Canadian Professional Golfers' Association for nearly three decades and first met Moe Norman in the early 1960s. Like Norman, Young has always been intrigued by metaphysics and has had access to the leading trance mediums. Young's brother is Neil Young, the internationally recognized singer-songwriter.